Printed by Amazon KDP.

ISBN 9781983281976

Content:

Chapter 1

Accelerating Change and the Luddite Threat

This is a declaration of a new politics. A politics designed for a world shaped by ceaseless technological change. It is a demand that we disenthrall ourselves of the Victorian political paradigm of left and right, and instead open our eyes to the true nature of today's global political struggle.

Today, technology is advancing rapidly. This rate of change is increasing exponentially and as it does it will fundamentally transform nearly every aspect of our lives.

This is not a new trend. It started when man first mastered fire and found the first sharp edge on a shard of broken flint. However, only as recently as the industrial revolution, with the power of the water wheel and the steam engine, did these forces become apparent and cause disruption over the course of an individual lifetime.

Today, life changing innovations are adopted and assimilated into our societies at breath-taking speed. The rapid invasion of personal computers into our homes, followed by their smart phone cousins into our pockets, has occurred, in historical terms, in the blink of an eye.

Changes are coming so thick and fast they are blurring into a continuum of constant change.

Until recently, politics has seemed indelibly structured around the perceived conflict between the haves and have nots, the owners of capital and the productive masses, the right and the left.

In fact, one does not need to succumb to communist dogma to acknowledge the nugget of truth in the Marxist maxim 'the history of all hitherto existing society is the history of class struggle'.

Whilst such an analysis may have been pertinent in the emerging industrial world, today everyone is engaged in a far more challenging struggle. Not against one another, but in response to the relentless advance of technology.

Personal wealth and privilege may help shield some individuals from the first ripples of this incoming flood. However, nobody will be able to shield themselves entirely from wave after wave of the coming powerful tsunami.

It could be said that the history of all hitherto existing society is the history of human adaptation to new technology. These transformative forces used to work over generations but now they are fundamentally recreating our world numerous times over in an individual lifetime.

It may appear self-evident that the rate of technological change is accelerating but it is important that the validity of this central premise is examined.

Change is driven by the creative energy of individuals and groups of people who can dedicate their time to developing new ideas. Looking back merely a few hundred years, the vast majority of individuals were tied to the land in every society. This was necessary in order for working people to sustain themselves, their families, the community and any extractive political organisations which preyed upon them.

Today, with improvements in agriculture and in global trade networks, fewer people are constrained in such a way. New roles have been created which help maintain our modern society but more people have been economically freed to take part in creative pursuits. To put this another way, there is enough surplus from the labours of a few to sustain a community increasingly engaged in innovation and development.

Educational opportunities were once only available to the privileged few yet increasingly, access to education is becoming widely available across the globe. More and more people are therefore able to contribute effectively to the global pool of scientific, technical or cultural knowledge. This increasingly means the location, culture or economic circumstances of an individual's birth will not prevent them exploiting their natural talents and abilities. There is still a long way to go before this is universally true. Nevertheless, as this expansion of participation continues, more creative time and energy will be invested in the economy.

It is also the case that modern processes of creativity and development are rarely individual pursuits. Instead, people with specialised knowledge and skills collaborate to create products that often could not have been conceived or brought into being by the necessarily limited capacities of an individual.

Global economic development, coupled with improved communications and transportation links, have allowed increased collaboration between people across the world from a wider range of economic and cultural backgrounds.

As these barriers separating the people of the world evaporate, and people are able to work successfully together, the opportunity will exist to make better use of every person's talents and potential. This will result in outcomes that could not have been achieved when people were operating in their former limited silos.

Finally, innovation is not generally a process of unique creation but instead a process of iterative improvement and recombination. Therefore, as the pool of human knowledge increases, so does the potential for new technological developments.

The ongoing development of information technology is a prime real life example of this process in action. Moore's law is an observation and extrapolation made in 1965 by Gordon Moore, who went on to become the co-founder of the American computer chip manufacturer, Intel. Gordon Moore observed that the number of transistors on an integrated circuit was doubling every year and he predicted that this trend would be likely to continue for the next decade.

With a small revision to the prediction in 1975, where he projected the doubling would occur every two years, Moore's law has held true for the best part of fifty years.

Whilst this trend is referred to as a law, evoking a sense of eternal progress and development in accordance with some universal and natural phenomena, the process will not continue indefinitely.

At some point, engineers will encounter physical barriers which cannot be overcome and it will become too costly or too difficult to pack more transistors onto a computer processor.

Nevertheless, the fact that for over fifty years this incredible rate of growth has been sustained is a testament to the creative abilities our economy can unleash.

The trend is not unique but thanks to the metric observed and defined by Gordon Moore, it is easily measurable. It is reasonable to conclude the focussed creativity of a dedicated global community, coupled with the necessary economic incentives, will always see such improvements until physical barriers are reached and it becomes less economically viable to push beyond them.

As innovation is driven through a process of recombination, this same trend in a number of key flagship industries creates waves of rapid improvements in many other industries that may not have initially seemed interconnected.

For example, many everyday items now have a microchip embedded within them to give the device some additional functionality and to help collate data about the products usage.

A mechanism has been described and an example provided by which widespread change could be accelerating. This has not, as yet, conclusively demonstrated this process is happening, nor has it shown such a trend is permanent and not a temporary era defined by a single, or group of, transformative technologies.

Therefore, it is necessary to acquire additional data which will allow us to infer this trend for longstanding accelerating change from other metrics.

According to data provided by the Organisation for Economic Co-Operation and Development, OECD, gross domestic spending on research and development within their member nations increased from just under 2% of Gross Domestic Product, GDP, in 1995 to just under 2.4% of GDP by 2015.

This seems like a fairly modest increase on first glance until the increases in average GDP within the OECD nations within this period are also reviewed.

This means gross domestic spending on Research and Development, R&D, in OECD nations rose from 604,447 million US dollars in 1995 to a staggering 1,143,005 million US dollars by 2015.

It can perhaps also be inferred that increases to total global GDP would also likely to be associated with, if not driven by, technological improvements as these developments increase productivity and generate value. Nevertheless, this must be decoupled from the proceeds of demographic growth as more consumers and world markets have opened up.

The rising costs of R&D does not necessarily indicate an increase of creative input into our economy as it could reflect the increased cost of even sustaining marginal improvements. The amount of creative output this investment is producing therefore needs to be assessed.

One may assume the rate of increase of patent applications submitted would be proportional to the rate of increase of technological development. After all, it is not unreasonable to assume the creators of these new technologies would wish to protect their intellectual property. As our model of accelerating change predicts, US patent statistics show a rapid increase in the number of applications being submitted. The number of patent applications has risen from just over 90,000 per year in 1963 to over 629,000 in 2015. That is over 1,725 patent applications a day and these are merely the products and developments which it was deemed worth taking out protection on. More strikingly, between 1995 and 2015, the numbers of applications have increased nearly threefold.

In addition to more applications for patents, the number of scientists this money is being used to support may help determine whether this additional investment results in a greater global creative capacity. Here again an accelerating trend can be observed.

In his book, 'Science Since Babylon', the science historian, Derek de Solla Prince, used the cumulative number of scientific journals found worldwide to project the number of active scientists. His graph demonstrated growth of approximately a factor of ten every fifty years between 1700 and the time of publication in the early 1960's.

Based upon the number of worldwide PhDs being granted annually, this trend is still broadly holding.

UNESCO, The United Nations Organisation for Education, Science and Culture, has reported a 23.4% growth in scientific publications worldwide between 2008 and 2014 including a 60% increase in Africa and an astounding increase of over 109% in the Arab states.

Such is the increase in the number of practising scientists, that approximately 90% of all of the scientists who have ever worked are alive today.

However, the individuals who are either contributing original papers to scientific publications or who have obtained PhDs, are only a small number of the people who are contributing creatively to our scientific understanding and technological mastery.

There are also a significant number of people worldwide who work in engineering or other technical professions not to mention the students, keen amateurs and garage innovators who contribute directly to the advance of technology.

Whilst these make up a compelling body of evidence, they are not definitive and qualitative measures of the nature of modern change. However, these examples should allow many to conclude the core assumption of this work is reasonable.

These forces are unstoppable and without compassion, care or motive. They will devalue our skills, turn once proud trades into the museum exhibits of the future and rip apart communities and established ways of life. Despite all this, they have the potential to be a considerable force for good.

Technological advance has the potential to provide untold opportunities. It will cure diseases, end absolute poverty, prevent wars and offer a plethora of technological wonders that can as yet barely be imagined.

The awareness of technological change as a political force already crops up within the political mainstream. It is generally presented alongside globalisation to explain a number of recent phenomena, such as the reduction in blue collar jobs within western nations.

In fact, in the 1960's, the preeminent economist, John Maynard Keynes wrote in an essay: 'I believe it is a widely mistaken interpretation of what is happening to us. We are not suffering from the rheumatics of old age but from the growing pains of over rapid changes from the pain of readjustment between one economic period and another.'

The failure to reframe our politics around this force and recognise that adapting to technological change is the new central challenge of our generation, if not every future generation, is causing an endemic political failure. This failure guarantees problems are being misdiagnosed and incomplete solutions are being offered to problems as they arise.

Instead of seeing technological advance as a peripheral issue which relates to a handful of isolated trends, the first relatively minor effects of this trend can be found at the heart of nearly all of the challenges faced by today's world.

The stagnation of wages; diminishing opportunities, in particular for young people; unemployment, underemployment and accomplished individuals unable to find productive applications for their skills; not to mention the growing and widespread political apathy as people feel powerless to control their lives and improve their personal circumstances; are all increasingly damaging forces within our societies.

These are no longer isolated political anomalies but are now part of a growing body of evidence that our present political paradigm is breaking down.

It is not that our politicians are disinterested or that they are not striving to stay in touch with the issues that are affecting our communities. Instead the lens through which they view the world is increasingly distorted and the apparatus at their disposal to resolve these issues is no longer fit for purpose.

It is time to refocus our political outlook around the single question: 'How should society react to the challenges created by ceaseless technological and allied social change?'

The problem is that such a task is far easier said than done. Firstly, political allegiances are strongly tied up with personal identity. They represent values and hopes for the future. These allegiances are often structured around a widely agreed and longstanding programme of measures which, according to each ideology, will deliver a better tomorrow.

In a world being shaped and reshaped around us every day, it is verging on ludicrous that our political debate is still largely centered on ideas which were formed over a century ago. A time before the widespread use of the telephone, let alone before smart phones had begun to connect every individual on the planet. A time before the first powered flight and long before the invention of the jet engine, which has opened up the world to mass, long distance travel and a time before the first electronic computer, which was overtaken by today's semi-conductor wonders.

In these new uncertain times, it is difficult to extrapolate trends even a short way into the future due to all of the complicated interactions between emerging technologies and the myriad of social and cultural reactions they generate.

Despite this uncertainty, many commentators have concluded that as a result of technological change there is a possibility of habitual unemployment for large swathes of the population as technology makes skills redundant and individuals' unemployable.

Such a dystopian future has not transpired to date despite rapid technological advance because developments have increased productivity and in return, this has increased demand which generates new jobs. In other words, such predictions may just be the modern expression of the Luddite fallacy. This may be good news for the economy but it does little to benefit the people who were displaced. These individuals can often struggle to reskill to take advantage of these emerging opportunities.

Our concern should therefore not be about the precise nature of the change, which to a large degree is unknowable, but instead our focus should be upon the challenges that will arise from the constant change and reinvention of society.

This would mean that even if people aren't falling permanently out of employment, they are constantly shifting and changing jobs making work and life far less consistent and predictable.

With the need to constantly restructure many parts of life, this is bound to bring about uncertainty which will lead to social and economic disruption. Despite the growing uncertainty and associated disruption, our politics and our institutions remain change-resistant and slow to recognise and adjust to a changing world. Hitherto, there were good reasons why this should be the case. Stability provides security and even well-meaning change can cause damaging and unforeseen consequences, especially if these changes were implemented without consideration or planning.

If change is so easy to make that a significant policy with wide-ranging economic consequences could be implemented, repealed, reinstated, amended and abandoned, as the political tide ebbed and flowed, a greater magnification of the disruption along the political cycle could be expected. Hence systems arose of checks and balances, consultation and debate and all this after the party of government had acknowledged the issue and proposed a solution in their election manifesto.

Changes in our economy, communities and society will soon no longer be a choice. It will not be led by our political institutions but instead it will be constantly imposed upon us by the unrelenting tide of technological change and there will be little time for hesitancy.

This need for the human mind to embrace a world which is ceaselessly changing around it and to constantly imagine new solutions is a new requirement and one the evolutionary process has had no need or means by which to prepare us.

To assume there would be no political response to these forces, implies society would be powerless or passive to any associated consequences. Fredrick Vinson, former US Secretary of State said: "What man has made, man can change." Despite the wisdom of these remarks, in our current political system, it would undoubtedly be hard to find the correct levers and pulling them may not cause an immediate response.

The political failure to recognise technological change as the new key shaping force within our society has ensured little action has been taken to reshape our institutions to be fit for purpose in the modern era.

As a result of this barrier to necessary widespread reform, growing political frustration can be observed. This growing frustration is exhibited with the rise of candidates who inhabit the political extremes. These individuals and the political movements they embody, promise a new political system which they claim will work for the people who feel they are being left behind.

Instead of recognising change and responding to it, these forces look to take sometimes radical steps to erect barriers to change, or even to wind back the clock. Whether that is building walls or building economic institutions to control or even stop change, these forces, even in their left wing expression, soon become extremely conservative.

They attempt to repress and control societies and maintain a world within which certain groups can remain comfortable, secure and even powerful. This is clearly recognisable as a Luddite approach. The Luddite movement arose when highly skilled textile workers in England in the 18th century recognised their livelihoods were under threat from new industrialised technologies. In response to this threat, they set about destroying industrial equipment and engaging in wider, and sometimes violent, protest. Similarly, a Neo-Luddite would feel threatened as the march of technological progress risked taking away the skills which provide them with their financial stability and security. Despite this similarity with their political forebears, a Neo-Luddite would be forced to resort to different tactics to stifle creativity as any attempts to damage or destroy technology would be futile.

This would principally be because the technological developments would not be confined to a region or two of one nation but instead will be distributed globally. It is also the case that with the growth of digital technology, a number of areas of our economy are non-rival which allows almost infinite copies to be produced and instantaneously distributed.

It is also likely that trades, skills or professions would no longer be under threat from one technology. Instead, an array of new innovations and developments may begin to infringe upon existing areas of employment and chip away at the value of hard-earned skills.

In order to slow the march of change, such Neo-Luddites would therefore need to implement a host of authoritarian measures and protectionist policies to halt development and innovation and isolate themselves from developments occurring in the outside world.

Failure to prevent communication would undoubtedly result in showcasing the technological advances, including important advances in fields such as healthcare, available in the outside world which would not be accessible to the repressed masses in our fictional Neo-Luddite nation. This would be akin to living behind the former Soviet Iron Curtain and seeing all of the developments that had happened in the West that were economically and socially out of reach.

Just as it did in the Soviet Union, this could only lead to a rise in discontent and a desire to change the political system to remove the barriers to these new wonders and opportunities.

But perhaps the worst consequence would be the loss of the wide range of advantages provided by the march of technological development if such a political system became dominant.

How different would life be today if 18th Century Luddites had been successful and the Luddite philosophy had swept across the globe?

Society wouldn't have the wonders of modern medicine or the financial means to support public healthcare systems. Working conditions would have remained poor with many people undertaking backbreaking and regularly unsafe labour. Increased educational opportunities would not have been afforded to millions which have in turn allowed many people to build a life based on their own ability and endeavour.

Put simply, the world is a better place for the failure of the Luddite doctrine. The same will be true of any future attempts to stop the hands of time by any group of people intent on protecting their advantage from the unrelenting technological change.

In fact, repressing change could also have more disastrous consequences than unleashing it. As a result of previous technological changes, there has been a dispersion of global wealth and opportunity reaching previously undeveloped nations. With modern communications and transport links, jobs can be offshored and outsourced around the world rapidly. Globalisation is increasing the standard of living in many developing nations, and whilst this process has only just begun, working people within the western nations are already feeling the effects of having many of their jobs offshored.

These losses initially occurred in manufacturing yet more recently this process has spread throughout the service industries. This is a positive situation in purely economic terms as it optimises the global labour force and it provides relatively high quality jobs in many developing nations. However, it is also a process which takes away the livelihood of those who once relied on these trades and professions for a decent standard of living.

If developed nations do not continue to be productive and creative they risk entering a spiral of reducing living standards as the wealth of the world becomes more evenly distributed across the globe.

The challenges around globalisation may provide the best glimpse of what the politics of a world of ceaseless change may look like.

There is no way of stopping globalisation without erecting barriers to trade, opportunity and innovation. Yet, anti-globalisation campaigns have been seen on both the left and right of the political divide. In fact, globalisation is itself a consequence of technological change which has removed the barriers that once protected vested interests in the developed nations.

The other problem is capitalist economies are built on the prospect and anticipation of growth. If there is zero growth or a retracting economy as a result of minimal technological development and barriers to trade then investor and consumer confidence collapses, spending halts and a period of falling incomes and rising unemployment could be expected.

Despite all of these clear disadvantages, such a damaging ideology may still take root. If people's skills, which they had worked hard to acquire, were being made redundant and if this risked taking away their family's financial security then perhaps a number of people may be willing to accept a more repressive political regime to prevent such outcomes. Increasingly people are choosing these political options, even though they are rarely presented as such. They feel something needs to be done to seize back control. They worry their children will have a worse standard of living than they do. They feel they have little ability to build and plan for the future let alone create a stable and successful career. This is understandably causing considerable distress and the feeling that the current political mainstream is no longer working.

Another approach must be explored. An approach which will recreate our institutions and reform our society to ensure people may build happy, worthwhile and prosperous lives in a world of relentless technological and allied social change.

In their book, 'Why Nations Fail', Acemoglu and Robinson, discuss at length how nations cease to be economically successful when their institutions become extractive. This process usually occurs under the direction of a narrow band of elites who wish to maintain their privilege and power.

In a world which is changing at an ever quickening rate, institutions cannot only become extractive because they have been designed to benefit a political elite, but also they can become extractive because they fail to adapt to changing social conditions.

In such a scenario, these institutions extract resources from society, resulting in diminished collective and individual economic freedom, without delivering for the public they were created to serve.

This does not have to be a malicious force but is sometimes the result of a natural human instinct to be change-resistant yet the same damaging economic and social consequences will ultimately follow. Such rigidity is therefore a damaging institutional force and a luxury that cannot be afforded.

Instead institutions must be designed to constantly adjust to the changing economic and societal conditions and dynamic systems need implementing which address problems as they arise.

Such an approach will be necessary as it will be nigh on impossible to foresee how technological changes will impact upon our society and our economy in the medium to long term.

Winston Churchill famously said: "We shape our institutions and then they shape us." Now each generation will shape and reshape our institutions and they will in turn shape and reshape us in an ongoing, accelerating cycle.

Yet there will remain no room for complacency. If institutions are designed to be truly open to change, there is a risk the system can quickly and easily be made less changeable by Luddite policies and proposals. Milton Friedman in his book 'Capital & Freedom' accepts capitalism allows people, through their individual economic freedom, to organise for a socialist system of government.

Whilst the author clearly believes communist ideas restrict freedom, he still supports the right of individuals to campaign for a socialist state. He recognises the nature of capitalism and individual economic freedom will provide access to opportunities such as the right to publish media which may further the socialist cause.

Friedman argues the same freedoms are unlikely to exist in extreme socialist economies for people attempting to argue for capitalist measures to be implemented.

In the same way, if additional freedom is provided to people to shape and reshape their society dynamically, so will the opportunity for people to exploit this new power to implement Luddite policies. These in turn are not only likely to restrict the freedoms of the next generation but also to repress the voices of those calling for more flexible and adaptable institutions.

This threat will ensure society can never be complacent about the security of any future dynamic organisations and the freedom they will help facilitate.

First however, our present institutions must be replaced, many of which have sustained themselves for hundreds of years with minimal reform. Just because an institution can sustain itself during this era of considerable social and economic change, doesn't mean it remains fit for purpose. Individuals are increasingly required to adapt to the changing world in order to achieve financial stability and access future opportunity. The same adaptability must now be demanded from our economic, political and social institutions.

Chapter 2

Dynamic Democracy and Decision Making

Anyone tasked with making a decision has to accept they do so in an uncertain world. Political decision making is no different. In fact, accelerating technological and allied social change means that the amount of uncertainty which must be tolerated in each decision is increasing. This makes the outcome of any decision less certain.

As only one version of history is experienced, it is difficult to determine if a chosen course of action delivered the best outcome of all possible worlds. Critics will therefore always be able to claim better decisions could have been made.

Whether or not the optimal outcome was achieved, this uncertainty means decision makers must expect continual criticism of the decisions they make.

Critical assessment is, and will remain, a vital part of any democracy. In today's world of twenty-four-hour news and social media, people are constantly inundated with reports and opinions on the performance of their policy makers. This can often be an important tool to hold politically influential people to account. It also can provide information which encourages members of the public to challenge perceived wisdom. Yet, there is little impartial analysis aimed at identifying instances, and the common traits, of quality decision making.

Such insight is surely fast becoming essential in a world which is generating new challenges as it quickly transforms around us. In the future, high quality decision making will have to occur considerably quicker than it does today. This will be necessary to prevent problems escalating to epidemic proportions before any necessary remedial action is taken.

It is therefore essential that the decision making process is carefully assessed. How can our current methods be amended and how can best practise be identified to ensure our decision making will be fit for purpose in an age of relentless change?

Political decision making is not just a single skill or attribute. Instead, all good political decision making can be broken down into four distinct components: Observation; prediction; vision and the chosen method of transitioning from the world as it is, or as it will be, to the world society collectively desires.

The starting point for good decision making is to have a set of clear and accurate observations.

The scientific method, which could be described as the process of unbiased, quantitative observation, has transformed our understanding of the natural world. From this foundation of solid observation, the technological revolution has been driven.

Despite modern society being built on accurate observation, many bad political decisions start out with observation seen through a prism of preconception or ideology. This often distorts and obscures our understanding of the world around us, allowing people with strong sets of preconceptions to become blind to evidence and information that does not fit neatly within their restricted world view. This is a process known as confirmation bias. Nobel Prize winning behavioural economist, Daniel Kahneman, writes in 'Thinking Fast & Slow': 'Contrary to the rules of philosophers of science, who advise testing hypotheses by trying to refute them, people seek data that is likely to be compatible with the beliefs they currently hold.'

People with such firm ideological beliefs, often become more confident in the accuracy of their understanding. This is generally because they have replaced the confusion and complexity of the real world with a simplified model they genuinely believe accurately describes the world around them. Such distortions are a continually disruptive force within our politics. Therefore, to reduce this effect, the vast majority of political parties who inhabit the ground to the left or right of centre, seek to build their policy from a foundation of empirical evidence collected both scientifically and independently.

However, there has been a worrying trend in recent times where observable evidence is being politically rejected. For example, the rejection by certain extreme groups of the overwhelming body of evidence from climate scientists, is a clear example of ideological blindness. Needless to say, future decision making quality will only be damaged if decision makers wilfully ignore independent observations and analysis.

In the past, when the rate of change was slower, it was sufficient to simply have good observations of the world around us as a solid foundation for good decision making.

The only necessary predictions were regarding the consequences and impact of a proposed political change. Therefore, it was usually sensible to ensure decision making was slow and considered.

Now it is essential to make rapid decisions. Situations can therefore not be allowed to develop before a reaction is considered.

Good decision making in today's world therefore relies on good predictions of the future.

Prediction however, is notoriously difficult. Contrary to popular expectations, few people are able to make consistently good predictions about the future and nobody can determine with certainty how events will develop.

This fact does not however prevent our political commentary being peppered with predictions, the quality of which are seldom assessed. It also doesn't mean prediction is a worthless endeavor if it is conducted correctly with a focus on improving forecasting accuracy.

Many people believe they have a good forecasting ability. Partly, this is because of the impact of hindsight bias. In 'Thinking Fast & Slow', Daniel Kahneman writes: 'A general limitation of the human mind is its imperfect ability to reconstruct past states of knowledge, or beliefs that have changed. Once you adopt a new view of the world (or any part of it), you immediately lose much of your ability to recall what you believed before you changed your mind.' 'Your inability to reconstruct past beliefs will inevitably cause you to underestimate the extent to which you were surprised by past events'

He continues: 'Hindsight bias has a pernicious effect on the evaluation of decision makers. It leads observers to assess the quality of a decision not by whether the process was sound but by whether the outcome is good or bad.'

The work of the Canadian-American Political Scientist and Psychologist, Philip E. Tetlock has helped shed some light on prediction accuracy of individual experts.

In his 2005 book, Expert Political Judgement: How good is it? How can we know? Tetlock presented an overview of his work principally looking at the accuracy of predictions of future real world events.

This work was derived from a study which looked at the predictions made by a number of professionals from different fields and from across the political spectrum.

Tetlock found expert forecasters were only moderately better at predicting events than if they had made a random prediction by chance.

Nevertheless, underlying this headline result was the observation that certain thinking styles delivered better results than others. Factors such as professional background or political outlook however, had no appreciable impact on predictive accuracy.

However, individuals who clung to one big theoretical idea or ideology and extrapolated this concept into other areas of knowledge had a far lower predictive accuracy than some of their counterparts.

Many people may have assumed more information would nearly always mean improved forecasting ability. However, Tetlock established additional expertise, above the level of a dilettante, did not deliver improvements in predictive accuracy.

The ability for an expert to draw upon a wider pool of evidence to back up their predictions can also result in excessive confidence in their conclusions. This can create a tendency to dismiss or ignore countervailing propositions. Unsurprisingly, experts, like any other individual, can become victims of confirmation bias.

Whilst individuals may make poor forecasters and poor judges of others forecasts, the predictive ability of crowds using aggregating methods such as decision making markets can deliver some impressive predictions.

It was once assumed large groups always diminished the intellectual ability of the individuals in the group. However, when the conditions are correct and the contributions of diverse and independent participants are properly aggregated, groups can have remarkable collective intelligence.

The useful information within a crowd starts out being distributed randomly amongst the members of the group yet these insights are often drowned out by the 'noise' of their individual errors and misconceptions. Individuals can make poor decisions as a result of cognitive biases, incomplete information, emotional factors and an inability to undertake complicated statistical calculations. Yet, the mistakes of an individual in a large independent group are likely to be cancelled out by the opposing mistakes of other participants within the group. This process therefore extracts and collates all of the useful information whilst removing errors which taint our individual analysis and assessment.

Many interesting examples of this phenomena are provided in James Surowiecki's excellent book 'The Wisdom of Crowds'.

Interestingly, there is also good evidence to show a group which seeks to incorporate wider opinions and diversifies to include people without formal expertise, sees improvements in decision making ability.

This is as a result of the wider range of experiences being drawn upon. Experts will generally emerge from, or coalesce into, a more homogenous group than the population as a whole. Therefore, they will be more influenced by their shared experiences and outlooks.

By widening the group, these diverse experiences and world views can supplement the information already in the system and can lead to better predictions and problem solving.

Despite these opportunities, such processes can dramatically fail if the individuals in a group have collective and systematic biases. Put another way, in cases where the participants' opinions have been generally skewed in one direction these errors no longer cancel out, but instead coalesce to provide misleading outcomes.

These are the conditions which are often found within a traditional political party. This is because members have self-selected as having broadly the same political outlook and are influenced within the organisation to conform to certain standard positions. A certain amount of skepticism should therefore be retained about decisions arrived at through collective processes within these groups.

Not all circumstances however lend themselves to crowd-sourced solutions. There may be situations where it is difficult to incentivise people to effectively participate or perhaps a mechanism could not be determined to successfully aggregate the information and insights of the crowd.

If crowd based solutions are unavailable to us in certain circumstances it is important to identify the conditions under which individuals are able to forecast successfully.

In 'Superforecasting: The Art and Science of Prediction'. Tetlock, along with his collaborator Dan Gardener, looked at individuals from the general population who exhibited the appropriate thinking style to deliver high quality real-world predictions. These people were termed 'superforecasters'.

These participants generally had the following attributes. They understood the complexity of the world and were able to express nuanced ideas laced with counterfactual points about how the future may develop. They were not constrained by their own ideologies or preconceptions and they were willing and able to collate and absorb information from a wide variety of sources.

Results were enhanced further when participants were grouped into 'superforecasting teams' and were provided with basic training exercises to help develop their probabilistic judgement.

By separating out the predictive process from elected officials and their internal teams of advisors, it should be possible to utilise their important insights without exacerbating the problems of political groupthink.

To maintain this separation and to ensure forecasters remain diverse and outside of direct political influence, a system should be adopted which is akin to the jury selection process. A random group of people from across society, who could demonstrate they possessed the correct thinking style, should undertake a short period of service to their nation or community by participating in forecasting teams.

Still, this will not provide a crystal ball to allow our political leaders to peer into the future. For any event which is neither certain nor impossible the only hope is to make an accurate probabilistic prediction of the event occurring. This will not tell decision makers categorically if an event will or will not happen.

A group of superforecasters or a crowd-sourced prediction could correctly inform political decision-makers a certain event was extremely unlikely, for example, it may only have a 1% chance of occurring. Yet, such an unlikely future may transpire.

This is not a failure of prediction. Unlikely events occurring or likely events not occurring cannot be perceived as proof that the predictive process is flawed.

Instead, there should be an expectation that an event with a 1% likelihood will occur 1% of the time and appropriate plans should be made in case the statistically unlikely, yet evidently possible, future occurs.

As a result, long range forecasts are not possible to make with any accuracy.

This is because future outcomes generally rely on a series of smaller events occurring or not occurring. This quickly increases the number of permutations of the future and the probability of each outcome quickly tends towards zero as each outcome relies on a large series of events all occurring as predicted.

The aim of our prediction is not to achieve perfect foresight. In reality, events do not unfold in a deterministic way into the future. Instead, the aim is simply to gain short term insights which will allow the opportunity to mitigate the forces of potentially damaging change.

Early insights and the opportunity for forethought will undoubtedly place us in a better position to ensure the consequences of fast moving, sweeping change can be addressed quickly.

Immutable predictions which do not change with events are therefore useless for our purpose. Political debate however is constructed around many of these longstanding ideological positions which are often unaltered by changing events and circumstances.

If a particular event occurs or does not occur, our model must adjust to determine and evaluate possible futures. New events are occurring in every corner of the world, every second of the day. Some of these events may be completely irrelevant to our model. Some may be immediately recognised as the dawn of a new social or economic epoch and some may appear inconsequential but on hindsight it may be realised one of these seemingly irrelevant occurrences triggered widespread and significant events.

Many events however will only become significant when coupled with thousands of other discrete, independent events and knowledge of all of these will be required to properly assess the incident's impact.

This information deficit is the reason why crowd based predictive methods such as decision markets should be preferred to determine outcomes. That being said, the aggregation methods and the incentives need to be carefully designed to ensure the data is not distorted. Even then, all of the information needed to make perfectly accurate predictions will not be available.

The third decision making consideration is the vision. Without an achievable, realistic and desirable agreed goal, society cannot make progress. Trying to do so would be akin to undertaking a journey with a number of people offering directions to an unknown destination. It will therefore be increasingly important for politicians to articulate clear visions for the nation, which can then be selected democratically.

Finally, the mechanism which takes us from the world as it is or how it may be, to the world we desire, as described by our political vision, must be determined.

Policy is however usually formed in two distinct yet equally flawed ways. Firstly, and most commonly, it is constructed by individuals or by fairly small groups of people. These decision makers are often members of the narrow political classes.

This speeds up the policy making process but these groups are rarely diverse. Therefore, because of their small size and homogeneity these decision makers have a narrow reference frame to draw upon.

This problem is exacerbated in groups with domineering leaders or steep hierarchies as subordinates feel less able to challenge the statements, ideas and preconceptions of their superiors. This further limits the information and insights available to the group.

Contact with people outside this group may of course help influence the group's outlook but the impact of such lobbying will be limited and will provide some groups with disproportional influence.

In contrast, policy can be formed collectively. Whilst this broadens the range of information available, it doesn't necessarily improve the policy making process.

As previously discussed, these groups within political parties can still be surprisingly homogenous and in order to conform to group expectations, opinions may be absorbed and regurgitated.

In addition, this process is undoubtedly slower than the small-group decision making model. In our age of change, can the time for these long consultative processes be afforded?

In many instances, for the large collective to decide to take action, a majority of the people involved must identify the issue as requiring action and agree on an appropriate solution.

Again, as the world transforms, is it acceptable and prudent to wait until a majority have identified and appreciated an impending challenge before acting?

Come what may, decision making cannot be a one-off process that takes place within an election cycle. The observation, prediction and policy making process must be constantly repeated to take into account changing circumstances. This will be the only way to prevent the delay from an issue being identified to a suitable solution being determined. Too often, solutions are already outdated before they have even been implemented.

If this is allowed to continue, problems may have already done considerable damage in the time taken for our political institutions to act. The initial problem may have subsequently transformed into an array of new problems which will require an entirely new set of political, social and economic reactions.

The former UK Prime Minister, Harold Wilson, allegedly once said; 'A week is a long time in politics.' This may have been a slight exaggeration when it was first uttered but not now as the rate of change continues to accelerate.

Certainly, waiting the best part of a decade for the current slow political process to play out is no longer appropriate or prudent.

This creates a rather difficult predicament. How are democratic ideals maintained whilst high quality decisions are made in a timely manner? The answer lies not by reaching consensus on a single course of action but instead to take multiple, varied approaches to the same problem. The conditions must be created where these solutions can compete in the real world to remain relevant to tackle social challenges and to earn and maintain popular support.

The ideas that flourish need to go and repopulate our institutional world with organisations and programmes that are fit for purpose in this new yet ever changing technological eco-system. In this way, solutions will evolve through a process akin to natural selection.

When fast ecological change happens, mass extinctions occur and there should be an expectation that policies and programmes will fall by the wayside in a similar manner.

This will not be indicative of failure but instead, it will show the system is working and is weeding out the ideas which failed to effectively meet a need. It will also remove policies or programmes where the problem vanished, transformed or failed to transpire leaving the solution redundant. Through the processes of competition and selection, our organisations will transition to become radically different from their predecessors.

This process must not be overseen and managed by a narrow group of decision makers. Just as government officials are not appointed to determine which crops should be grown in certain fields or which factories should manufacture certain products, our policy making should be handed over to the crowd.

Therefore, new political institutions are required which are effective aggregators of collective wisdom. These systems must be able to pull together the important insights and snippets of knowledge which exist within the population at large. Only in this way will it help us achieve better decision making outcomes.

The risk is of course that decisions would be made and nobody would seem to be accountable. Mistakes which did occur could appear faceless and this could cause significant distress to individuals caught up in any negative consequences. Nevertheless, whilst it may not be as easy to assign blame to a particular individual in such a system, decisions would be transparent and would have achieved some form of public consent.

However, it is clearly important that immoral or amoral proposals are not allowed to be implemented because nobody is shouldering the responsibility and burden of the final decision. This responsibility must still remain with elected political leaders. In addition to setting the collective vision of a nation or community, they must also redefine their role to provide the final check on the policy proposals generated by the crowd. This is not a new idea and would be akin to the oversight which exists in financial markets to prevent immoral or exploitative trading practises.

A practical example of such a proposal could be a system which allowed tax payers to allocate the value of their personal tax contribution dynamically to government programmes, projects or proposals of their choice.

A number of proposals should be perpetually sourced which it was believed could help achieve an agreed goal from our present starting point. A nation's political leaders would then need to ensure the apparent outcome would be consistent with the agreed vision and the proposals were not morally abhorrent. Assuming these two criteria were met, the crowd could allocate their resources to the projects which they believed would be the most beneficial.

If a certain project appeared to be delivering positive outcomes, more individuals would allocate their resources to this project allowing it to grow in scope. However, as it became apparent a once successful organisation was now floundering, its funding should dry up and be reallocated dynamically to some of its up and coming competitor institutions.

In addition to the benefits of crowd sourced decision making, such a system of allocation would give each individual tax payer more confidence their hard earned money was going to deliver services which were making a positive social contribution.

Instead of people pushing back against even moderate tax rises, this may increase confidence in public expenditure and result in individuals being more willing to allocate a larger proportion of their income to these collective community projects.

In other markets, participants are incentivised for allocating resources to their preferred service by receiving the product or service they either desired or determined was the optimum option. This is not, and should not be, the same for public services. In this instance, members of a community are not determining the services they will personally gain access to but instead they are allocating funds that, along with the funds of others, will provide programmes which will be available to anyone who requires the service.

It is therefore essential a situation does not arise where people must allocate purely for their own personal access as public services should be based upon need and not upon the ability to pay. Other forms of incentives are therefore required to make sure people are encouraged to allocate their resource effectively to projects in the public good.

A system is needed which assesses the quality of individual public investments and rewards individuals whose investments have made a positive contribution to achieving our collective goals. To do this, a number of metrics must be identified which will provide an accurate and comparable assessment of the impact of each individual policy programme. Using this data, a system which rewarded individuals whose investments were delivering positive outcomes should be designed and implemented. For example, people who have invested wisely for the social good should receive a deduction from their future personal tax contribution.

If designed correctly, such incentives could be raised and lowered dynamically by sector to encourage investment in positive and innovative institutions and programmes in the areas of the most significant public need.

Such a system however, may create more uncertainty within public sector employment due to the constant change it will encourage. However, as well as transferring resources to competitor services, it will also motivate existing public sector bodies to positively transform themselves. This will be essential so they remain relevant, fit for purpose and efficiently meeting a public need so as not to risk their funding collapsing.

After all, many of our successful businesses are constantly undergoing a similar process of regeneration and as a result are able to offer well paid and stable employment because the business continues to be competitive. Even with proper incentives in place, some people will not allocate their funds optimally or even wisely yet from this unstructured melee of personal preferences and insights, we should expect useful information to emerge from the system.

This process can be observed in action every day. For example, when new business opportunities open up, the market is flooded with a wide variety of products designed to meet this new need.

After the World Wide Web was first developed by Sir Tim Burners-Lee in 1989, it became apparent search was going to be a vital component to make the web more accessible. A considerable number of search engines became available with solutions such as Lycos, Yahoo! and AltaVista dominating the early market. New and unique search tools kept emerging but there was little consensus about which site to use to efficiently find the desired pages. Then, in 1996, Larry Page and Sergey Brinn founded Google after developing the 'Page Rank' algorithm at Stanford University.

Overtime, more people discovered they achieved better search results with Google in comparison to other search engines and Google increased their market share.

Google of course did not rest there. At the time of writing the company have over 4.5 billion active users. This is because it has continued to improve and transform the search algorithms and tools available to its users to ensure it maintained its market advantage. If Google had ceased to innovate after 'Page Rank' it would have been superseded and another search engine would now be our main portal to the plethora of information now available on the web. This process will never cease and neither should our policy making processes.

Nobody decided centrally that Google should be the search engine of choice for the vast proportion of the world's population. However, simply through a process of individual choice, competition and investment, a good solution has been found to the problem of web search.

If it had been up to a central commissioning body instead of a market, such an efficient search tool would not be at our disposal. This could have meant that the web would not have developed into the useful or transformative technology it has become.

Nobody believes failed start-up businesses are damaging the economy. Instead these alternative products and business models are part of the selection process which delivers successful organisations which help meet societal needs and desires. The same outlook and acceptance of the need for trial and error should exist when forming policy. Undoubtedly there will be an element of wastage as the investment in the failed systems will have not delivered a positive outcome. However, there are undoubtedly unproductive or at the very least suboptimal solutions which are currently in place in our institutions but these forms of wastage are often not actively removed by our current system.

Some people may recoil at the prospect of putting a system with market properties at the centre of our public decision making process. However, this is not a system designed to allow a small number of people to extract resources from our valued public services. Instead it would be a system designed to truly democratise decision making by allowing everybody to contribute to these decision making markets. Just as the 'invisible hand' ensures the market can rapidly adjust to meet changing demand, our system will ensure our society can adjust to changing need.

That being said, in certain areas, such an approach would be confusing and frankly dangerous if competing policies were encouraged. For instance, in areas of foreign policy where it would not always be possible to pursue simultaneous policies of appeasement and conflict against aggressive world powers. Evidently, such circumstances need identifying and, after considering our observations and predictions, a consensus position needs to be reached before a single course of action is taken. When it comes to creating legislation, it is also essential there remains one clear set of rules to operate by. It isn't possible to have competing statutes which could be selected at will. It is also the case that such legislation must have popular consent for people to retain respect for the law. Therefore, the opportunities for dynamic legislation are limited. This will probably mean, as the pace of change increases, legislative change will become a less powerful tool to address rising social challenges. It will still be necessary to legislate to meet changing societal demands and expectations but dynamic programmes and institutions will soon provide far more timely protection and support in an ever changing world.

To summarise, our political decision making processes need transforming in the following ways:

It is essential to push back against attempts to remove or undermine independent and scientific observation as the starting point for good policy making.

Sensible crowd sourced prediction methods should be introduced where possible, which dynamically adjust to changing conditions. Where this is not possible, an independent predictions service should be established outside of political influence which will assess information and trends and determine probabilities of events occurring.

Political leaders must set clear visions of the future which the population as a whole can select democratically.

New and inclusive policy making processes must be developed where individuals and groups suggest and select an array of solutions to tackle mounting problems and to seize new opportunities.

Finally, our elected representatives must act as a safety net to ensure these proposals will help achieve our collective aims and the measures are morally acceptable.

Needless to say this is a huge transformation from the current political decision making process but a fast moving system of competition and selection will almost certainly deliver improved outcomes. It will give the wider public a better understanding of how and why errors have occurred and provide more immediate tools at their disposal to put things right. Without question, people will lose trust in politics if these changes aren't made as the current political systems will not be fit for purpose to meet their needs as they arise.

Now is the time to transition to a dynamic democracy before the consequences of inaction get progressively worse and people lose even more faith in the current, outdated political model.

Chapter 3

Skills Decay and Career Change

Pick up a book about the technologies of the future and there will almost certainly be a chapter discussing technological unemployment.

No matter the specific technology under the spot light, the conclusion remains the same. The job prospects and job security of nearly every working person are under threat.

However, this is not a new idea. Creativity is destructive. The old is swept away by the new and with this, specific jobs will undoubtedly disappear as they have in the past and as they surely will again in the future.

This process of technological unemployment has been recognised for generations. The introduction of mechanisation and automation both generated considerable and justified concern.

Without question it is true the introduction of a new technology can create short term job losses. This often means workers who find their skills have been undermined do experience real and often painful consequences. Nevertheless, generally the benefits of improved efficiency and growth have resulted in new and generally better paid jobs arising in developing areas of the economy.

The success of these compensation effects has resulted in concerns about future joblessness to be termed 'The Luddite fallacy'. Thankfully the predictions of an economic and social apocalypse have not as yet materialised. In fact, the opposite has been true. Global living standards have continued to rise and the modern global economy supports more people than ever before.

That being said, a number of techno-profits are willing to overlook this historical trend. They believe and eagerly forecast a number of factors relating to the nature of modern technological change will mean this age old prediction will cease being a fallacy and will become a depressing fact of the future.

If our central premise is correct, that the rate of technological and allied social change is accelerating, it is easy to conclude the rate of job destruction and creation will also continue to accelerate. This will mean at the very least, more career churn and with it more uncertainty for hard working people and their families.

New technologies of any description have the opportunity to create the demand for new jobs in our economy as productivity is improved, money is saved and the creative energy of more working people can be directed to meet new or latent demands and desires. Yet this is only applicable if people are able to adjust and adapt to the new careers before these emerging opportunities are also swept away by the next technological or social change.

Technology is not necessarily a job killer but the rate of job churn will be the real concern for many working people.

As this rate of churn continues to accelerate, there will likely be widespread uncertainty in the job market and this clearly will have a considerable negative economic effect. If a steady income cannot be secured, a rational person would cease spending on all but the essentials. It would be prudent to save for the periods in the future when they became unemployed or had to accept a job in a new field with significantly less remuneration.

An individual would be unlikely to borrow in these circumstances, making large ticket purchases almost impossible for all but the wealthiest households. In short, large numbers of people could stop being effective consumers. Such a trend would slow job creation and the economy could risk entering a depressing spiral of decline.

Make no mistake, in the not too distant future, every job which exists today will either have disappeared from the jobs market or it will have transformed to require an entirely new set of knowledge and skills. Therefore, how people transition between careers and how they retain some certainty and security and their lives needs to be carefully looked at.

In 1789, Benjamin Franklin famously wrote: 'In this world, nothing can be said to be certain except death and taxes.' Assuming some truth in this maxim, the only certain careers in a world transforming around us would therefore perhaps be the role of an undertaker and a tax collector.

In days gone by this may have been accepted and people would have probably been able to reel off a list of other apparently eternal and immutable careers. Not in today's world.

It only takes a moment to imagine how these careers may transform or disappear in the not too distant future.

In the last decade, physical money has started to be replaced by electronic transactions and it is easy to imagine cash will soon be entirely replaced. When this occurs and every transaction can be monitored, the role of the taxman will surely be replaced by an algorithm which will automatically deduct and credit accounts in line with the tax code. No more errors. No more opportunity for tax avoidance and a once stable career will have vanished.

Robotic undertakers may not as yet be socially desirable but technologically it is within the reach of modern robotics and it is perhaps one more undesirable job a machine can assume.

This observation has not been made in order to predict the imminent end of these careers. However, in a world driven by technological change, acquiring a set of skills, whatever they may be, does not guarantee a stable career. Everyone is a technological development or social change away from finding their skills have become redundant.

In fact, instead of viewing skills being one development away from redundancy, skills should be thought of as constantly decaying over time. All knowledge has a half-life of productive value and that half-life is rapidly decreasing.

Clearly, the value of some skills does increase. This must be the case as any new skill starts without any value and increases over time to eventually support a group of workers within a trade or profession. Therefore, the following processes must be taking place:

Firstly, a skill may become more valuable when grouped with other complimentary skills to create a more defined role or trade. Secondly, technological advances may bring down the cost of component parts or associated services and this may bring a particular skill into the economic reach of more people. Similarly, if wages rise in society, the potential consumer base for a product or service could grow. Demographic growth, either from the expansion into new markets or from an expanding population in an established market will also provide more potential customers for a specialised skill.

Lastly, fashions and trends can change making a skill more desirable but this process can act in both directions with some products and services quickly becoming undesirable as fashions change.

All of these factors, increase the total amount of potential value accessible within a particular trade.

Now, consider a scenario where the skill in question, whilst gaining widespread value, can be acquired nearly immediately by any member of the population.

As the value within the trade goes up, the number of people competing to apply this skill also increases. They share out this increase in value and wages stay low. Anyone seeking to demand a higher wage could simply be replaced by an individual willing to work for less.

Despite the total value of the trade increasing, the average amount of value that can be extracted by an individual with the particular skill in question is not increasing. However, not all skills can be so easily acquired. If a skill is scarce and will require a considerable educational investment from other working people or there are other barriers to participation, more value can be extracted from this skill as demand will outstrip supply for longer.

However, in a world of constant change, this surplus of eager consumers and deficiency of skilled providers cannot last long. In such a scenario, there would be considerable economic incentives for any individual who could mechanise or automate the process. If such automation was successful, it would reduce the value that can be extracted by the skilled person in two ways. Firstly, such developments will increase the amount of work that can be done by a single operative or team of operatives using the machine which would perhaps remove some of the scarcity value. Secondly, the skill has now begun to transform. The original skill may no longer be useful as the role now needs an individual to competently operate the tool, device or machine. This ensures working people will need to undertake some form of reskilling to remain in the trade. This has clearly devalued the original skill.

Competition is not just taking place between individuals who may be able to undertake a specific task more efficiently and productively. As a result of constant technological change, competition also exists with alternative products and services which will constantly be spilling onto the market. Even if a trade is resistant to change, it does not mean consumers will continue to select the pre-existing products or services when they encounter a vast array of new choices.

Whilst the processes of market growth and the inelastic response of the Labour market may have in the past, increased the extractible value of a skill in the short run, this has never been the case over the long run.

Today, our skills decay before our eyes. They have a half-life of usefulness and the average half-life is decreasing. Skills decay has always occurred but often these changes were invisible in the short length of a human life span until the industrial revolution brought them into the range of a working lifetime.

This applies to all trades yet some skills decay quicker and some slower than others depending upon the cultural and technological pressures.

When a trade stops incorporating new skills, this generally starts a process of decline which eventually ends up with the trade disappearing or supporting a small number of artisans who maintain the craft for the niche consumer.

Either way, the ability to extract value from an unchanged set of skills decreases over time. In twenty years, it is hard to predict how any modern industry will have changed but it is safe to say it will have either continued to transform at an ever accelerating rate or it will have stagnated and the industry will be in an unstoppable decline towards being a lost art or tomorrow's museum exhibit. This is the life-cycle of every skill or trade and all of our jobs are vulnerable to these forces.

This life cycle is now being compressed into an ever decreasing time period. New technologies arrive, usually with lots of different competitive iterations, compete in the market to exist which the strongest propositions quickly dominate before being widely adopted. Before long the technology underpinning the industry is superseded, the consumer's expectations or desires change or jobs start being removed as the process is mechanised or taken over by algorithms.

In addition to this insecurity created by the decay of profitable skills, the job market in a world of rapid technological change creates another dilemma for would-be workers.

Increasingly, due to the complexity of the modern world, it is essential to specialise in order to secure skilled and well paid work. Specialisation requires a large investment of time and energy, not to mention the opportunity cost of acquiring alternative and potentially lucrative skills. However, in the modern world, this can be a risky investment. As the world transforms quickly, there can be no guarantee an acquired specialisation will have a useful application in the future.

If a financial investment was made in, for instance, risky start-up businesses, the investor would be encouraged to diversify their investment portfolio.

This is clearly sensible. If lots of small investments are made in companies which have a low success rate but would deliver considerable returns, there remains a good chance of making a reasonable overall return. There is still risk but by diversifying investments the danger associated with a one off investment reduces.

It is therefore perhaps sensible to also diversify an investment in skills. However, anyone undertaking training only has a limited amount of time to invest in learning opportunities. Therefore, by failing to focus an investment of time in one particular group of skills, it becomes impossible to specialise.

Value in society is heavily dictated by scarcity. If there is a scarce yet desirable skill, anyone possessing that skill can command a good wage for their labour. If however a skill is abundant in the job market, competition between workers will drive down the value of this work to the socially agreed base level, a minimum wage, or it will tend to zero. This process will only stop when it ceases to be economically viable for any worker in any part of the world to undertake this task.

So what is the optimum strategy for acquiring well paid work? Some may gamble on one particular specialisation and it might pay off in a big way. More however will find their considerable investment of time and energy provides no economic benefit or only maintains a short burst of profitable employment before they re-joined the masses of unskilled, low paid workers.

Some may opt for a general approach to learning and may even argue, in a world being taken over by task specific application and even robots, future jobs will be based on a person's flexibility, general intelligence and broad application.

New technological tools are transforming jobs which once required specialist skills into trades accessible at the touch of a button. For example, it used to take teams of experts months to produce films or television programmes. Now, films are being shot and edited on smartphones with next to no training.

Different strategies will be more or less successful in different industries depending on their rate of transformation, the risk of automation and the scale of the skills investment required to operate successfully in the industry. However, as previously stated, value in a market is always proportional to scarcity. The global economy has nearly always operated with a labour surplus and rarely with a jobs surplus. In fact, whenever such surpluses existed in a particular country, nations would generally relax immigration controls and the surplus of workers would be increased.

However, the job market is not currently configured in a manner which means any worker can fill any position due to many roles requiring high levels of specialisation in order to be conducted correctly. This feature of specialisation is not only therefore a more efficient way of utilising labour but it also ensures the likely scarcity of a specific skill or set of attributes. This helps retain the value of the skill or trade. Alternatively, a global workforce of generic workers will not only fail to meet the needs of the future economy but it will ensure the vast majority of labour has no scarcity power and wages will undoubtedly fall accordingly.

However, even if an individual pursues the optimum skills strategy and they are fortunate enough their skill doesn't decay too rapidly to the point of redundancy, the concept of the standard vertical career path will still need adjusting.

Hitherto, people would expect to start a career and climb as far as their talent and good fortune allowed up an existing and predictable career ladder. Nowadays, the perception of what a career will look like must change to include more lateral and even backwards steps as people traverse a far less linear career path.

Rapid technological change will undoubtedly result in an economy in constant flux and therefore the skills and knowledge in demand throughout our working lives will regularly shift. This will put pressure on employment and such forces are already being seen in action with the emergence of the 'gig economy'.

Increasingly, employees are not being treated like a vital cog in a machine but instead like computer hardware components which can be clipped in and out to upgrade or amend the purpose of the machine. This might make good economic sense for employers but it means an entirely new framework of worker's rights will be required to ensure people are not exploited or forced to work in hazardous conditions.

This will mean in addition to addressing eroding wages and a lack of job stability, it will be essential to focus on protecting working rights. These were won and improved over time thanks to strong and effective Trade Unions. Yet these proud and vital institutions are under pressure from a number of forces. Shorter average periods of employment in different jobs prevent workers building the trust and support of their colleagues essential for collective action.

Trade Unions organise in workplaces and require a certain proportion of representation or a recognition agreement to negotiate on behalf of their members. How should this be changed if employment is far more variable?

Furthermore, existing rules mean workers' rights often do not apply for an initial period after employment. For example, in the UK there is currently a two-year qualification period for the majority of working rights. In a world of constant change, this could soon mean nobody has rights as more and more people spend careers leaping from job to job and the ability of trade unions to represent and defend their members is diminished.

Contracts without any fixed or guaranteed hours are used by employers in many low skilled industries to allegedly improve their flexibility. In a world of ceaseless change, this might seem prudent for an employer but it also results in the employee having no effective working rights as each employee has no entitlement to any hours of employment and pay.

Finally, how is it possible to distinguish between unnecessary cost-cutting and legitimate changes which may be needed to meet the transforming needs of the business or organisation?

The former is a cynical action at the expense of dedicated employees who have contributed to the growth and stability of the company. The latter would arguably help secure the future of the workforce as a whole.

These are monumental challenges for a movement which has undergone little change since its creation in the midst of the industrial revolution but they won't be solved by the movement becoming a barrier to inevitable change. The Trade Union movement needs a new, clear focus on improving opportunities and economic stability for members as they inevitably move between careers and employers or need to fundamentally reskill whilst in work.

Swathes of working people will lose out if the trade union movement fails to adapt to the nature of the new economy and jobs market. However, new legislation will also be required and new ideas will be needed to help provide safety, security and fairness in such a volatile job's market.

As employers attempt to divest themselves of their responsibilities to their employees and as periods of employment reduce, individual working people will not significantly benefit from the success of the company their endeavour is helping to build. This will undoubtedly shift the balance in the rewards distributed between capital and labour.

Therefore, in order to allow hard working people to share in the rewards of an organisations success, a method is required through which the workforce can obtain an ownership stake.

One solution to this volatile jobs climate, which is often discussed, is the Universal Basic Income (UBI). A UBI is a system where each member of a society is allocated a flat rate starting income which can be topped up with earnings.

In a job market defined by ceaseless technological and social change, a UBI could clearly have some advantages. This however should not be presented as a panacea to solve the employment challenges linked to widespread poor job prospects, poor wages and poor job security.

An economic safety net will be insufficient if people lose the dignity associated with earning a wage and supporting themselves and their loved ones.

If individuals lose the positive stimulation work provides and if the hope that comes from having the ability to improve one's standard of living through work is taken away, a UBI will provide little comfort.

Instead of a universal income, a guaranteed universal investment would perhaps be a better system of redistribution, not just of wealth but also of opportunity by providing working people with a capital stake in organisations of their choice. This proposal will be reviewed in more detail in the following chapter.

Another interesting variant of a UBI was trialled successfully in Uganda where the government provided a cash lump sum with no strings attached to every school leaver who submitted a business plan. No follow up or assessment, no requirement to repay and no targets to hit. Just opportunity for anyone willing to take it.

This idea should be extended. Every person, on reaching the age of 21, should receive a bond of considerable value which could be used to start a business, to build an investment portfolio or could be saved to pay off university tuition fees or put down a first deposit on a house.

Such a 'universal opportunity bond' for all 21 year olds could perhaps be funded by increasing inheritance tax.

People need access to money when they are young to create opportunities for themselves yet often, inheritance arrives when they too are reaching or have exceeded a pensionable age and when they are usually relatively financially secure.

The big discrepancy in wealth distribution is therefore not simply between classes but instead it is often between generations.

Now clearly, many older people have worked a lifetime so they have a degree of financial security in their golden years and it would be undesirable to take this away. However, by effectively releasing their equity contained in their property and assets and by redistributing this to the young generation, it would allow older people to enjoy their retirement whilst seeing their grandchildren equipped with the resources they need to thrive.

An entire generation could be moved out of poverty at the start of their working lives. Whilst some may slip back, this start in life will surely help the vast majority of people to build successful and positive lives instead of being constantly stuck in the poverty trap.

No proposal is entirely without costs and it is only appropriate to consider these. By funding this system through a process of equity release of estates, it may compel some people to divest themselves of their asset wealth and instead consume heavily in the last few years of life. This is not necessarily a negative for society as it would allow older people to benefit fully from their lifetime of hard work instead of feeling the need to hoard a proportion of this wealth for the benefit of their children. The main losers would clearly be those likely to inherit large sums as this amount would be reduced, particularly if such a scheme had a redistributive element built in.

However, their children would have benefited from the bond as they are starting out on their career journey instead of at a time of their lives where their expenditure was reducing. The current average inheritance age in the UK is 53 which is after the time most individuals have to set up a home or cover the costs for their children.

People are rightly more risk averse as they are preparing for their retirement years. This 'advance' on inheritance therefore increases the usefulness of this capital as the younger generation will be motivated and able to seize opportunities which will help generate a longstanding return. Alternatively, as inheritance tax is historically unpopular and difficult to collect, the aforementioned Universal Investment could be allocated to each citizen from birth but not paid out until the individual reaches twenty-one when the total amount accrued would be awarded as a lump sum.

The Opportunity Bond coupled with the regular Universal Investment, covered in more detail in the following chapter, would effectively mean every person will be provided with both the seed capital to set up a business and an investment to either sustain their own businesses or to invest into other start-up or established businesses.

In summary, the working lives of the next generation will bear little resemblance to the careers of their parents and grandparents. Not only will their jobs be entirely different but they will follow far more erratic career paths as they move between fleeting opportunities. Nevertheless, if people have the tools and resources to grasp opportunity, develop their skills and share the proceeds of capital, an economy could be built which works for working people.

Chapter 4

Economic Uncertainty and Competition

with the Future.

Today every person is engaged in a struggle. Not against one another, but

in response to the relentless advance of technology. This statement can be

made because the impact of technological change will not only impact

labour but it will also have a considerable impact upon the owners of

capital and our financial institutions.

Whilst the impact upon labour has been well recognised, it could be

argued the owners of capital have presently benefitted from technological

advance. For instance, capital's share of income has been steadily rising

over recent years.

The capitalist economy relies on the promise of constant growth generated by new products and services and by improvements in productivity. Sometimes, during periods of war or recession, this condition is not temporarily met but in the long run consistent and long term growth powered by technological change has been observed for the best part of two centuries.

Growth is important for a number of reasons. It helps maintain investor confidence and business investment in research and development. It increases tax revenues which can be invested in improved public infrastructure and services and it potentially increases consumer spending power. All of this helps generate future growth.

Perhaps then, at the heart of a prediction of accelerating technological growth, there is also the promise of eternal economic growth as productivity is improved and the value of individual products and services increases.

John F. Kennedy popularised the saying 'A rising tide lifts all boats' which implies improving economic conditions will be to the benefit of all. Whilst such an opportunity exists, it would be dangerous to assume these benefits cascade from continuous technological development.

As demonstrated in the previous chapter, the labour market, might fail to be an effective distributor of wealth. If unaddressed this could lead to social tensions and a dangerous neo-luddite reaction. It is therefore important to consider who the principal beneficiaries of this new abundance will be.

Secondly, accelerating technological change does not result in the expectation of ever rising rates of growth.

Developed nations have only seen on average 2% growth each year for the best part of 150 years despite clear acceleration of technological change during this period.

This is because of the cumulative nature of growth. Growth of 2% in 1775 would have been considerably less additional wealth than 2% growth in 2015. This is because the total size of the 1774 economy was so much smaller than the 2014 economy. In fact, technological and demographic growth need to accelerate exponentially to maintain a flat growth rate. Each technological development does not simply add value into an economy but it also destroys value. Therefore, the total growth observed, minus the demographic growth, is equal to the value of a technological development less the value of the industries which can no longer compete or generate desirable goods in this changed market place. This constrains the levels of growth that should be expected.

Only developing countries who can copy the successful developments in more technologically advanced nations get to achieve growth rates higher than the 2% average achieved in Europe and North America.

Growth is not only the result of new products, technologies and associated productivity increases but it is also driven by growth of population. This provides more people to undertake productive work and more consumers to buy global produce. Globalisation has continued to open up more markets for products and has helped deliver the technologies to other countries which allow their workers to be more productive.

However, both of these forces are coming to an end. Studies have predicted global population will rise to around 9.6 billion before stabilising around the year 2050. In addition, the vast majority of the world has opened up to trade opportunities and many of these developing nations are experiencing fast economic growth. This has already converted many of their citizens into effective global consumers.

It should therefore be expected the 2% average growth rate observed in developed nations over the last 150 years should reduce in the future as few additional gains can be made through demographic growth.

With low future economic growth rates expected, even a small amount of inflation could devalue capital assets and retained wealth over time. It is therefore important to look at likely inflationary and deflationary pressures in the future to determine the risk to capital.

Assuming consumer spending power in the future is not curtailed by poor wealth distribution and a lack of opportunities across society, then globalisation will quickly expand the number of active consumers. Soon there could be close to 10 billion people competing for products and services.

Whilst many of these products and services may be non-rival, some products will undoubtedly be limited in some way and demand may exceed supply. This will either be due to the time taken to scale production or due to a lack of particular natural resources. This creates the potential for demand-pull inflation as the world's population of consumers compete to obtain these desirable yet in some way limited products.

This potential inflationary pressure is not a direct result of technological change. It is however a second order effect resulting from technological change breaking down barriers to trade, transport and communication which has allowed globalisation to occur rapidly.

Governments and central banks have focused in recent years on keeping inflation low for a number of important reasons.

They have done this principally by limiting money supply. This not only slows consumer demand and with it demand-pull inflation but it also makes less capital available for investment in new technologies and new jobs. This slows the pace of change which may seem desirable but applying this break only holds up development in the western world whilst the developing world continues to advance rapidly. Such measures therefore limit new job opportunities for working people in the former leading nations who are seeing their old jobs being rapidly offshored. Such processes have helped undermined the consumer base in western nations who over recent years have borrowed to maintain their consumer spending power. They have been able to do this partially as a result of the cheap credit that low and stable inflation rates have helped provide.

However, this cannot continue indefinitely. If job stability and wages are continuously diminished, then low borrowing rates will not be enough to maintain any degree of consumer spending and growth.

In an economy and society in constant change, overall demand has to increase to ensure there remains enough interested consumers to acquire the plethora of new products and services being generated by the market. Perhaps some people will conclude limiting consumer power will be the best way to limit the pace of change. However, if growth is limited and people cannot afford to consume beyond their current means, investors will cease to provide capital for static returns and before long a spiral of economic decline has begun that could be difficult to halt without finding a method to once again kick start spending.

A system is required to control inflation without using the break of monetary policy which also curbs technological development and with it growth. Fortunately, rapid technological change may in fact automatically counteract inflationary forces without the need for another mechanism. Moore's law, introduced in Chapter One, is not just an example of technological acceleration but also a good example for technological deflation. Another way of stating Moore's law would be that the cost of maintaining the same processing power halves every two years. This helps demonstrate, as a result of technological advance, the price of existing technology decreases dramatically with time.

Deflation has been something governments and central banks have also worked hard to address and considerable amounts of work is done to make sure early signs of a deflationary trend are noted and not allowed to take root. This is a result of consumer psychology. If prices are likely to be cheaper tomorrow it is rational to defer spending. If enough customers defer spending then this can cause an economic shock where businesses can no longer achieve the necessary sales of their products. This results in job losses and with these more consumers are lost and this impacts other businesses.

However, technological advancement always means that every day a consumer defers a purchase, they are going to be able to acquire more technology for their money. This is clearly a threat to any organisations which operate in this domain.

Present metrics do little to quantify this process. The Consumer Price Index (CPI) is calculated by comparing standard shopping baskets of goods and services. However, these shopping baskets have to change over time due to technological advance and changes in social preferences. This need to change the contents of the shopping basket will only accelerate as technological change accelerates making the ability to compare like with like all the more difficult. In fact, the methodology, whilst understandable as consumer habits change, disguises this form of deflation.

It is also perhaps a more accurate reflection of the experience of many consumers, many of whom may report they have not seen any reductions in prices. This is due to the fact that whilst the products of yesterday have devalued, it is increasingly important to have access to the cutting edge products and services available to prevent social exclusion.

Whilst deflation has the potentially damaging economic consequence discussed, it is fundamentally something which is positive to the consumer. If an individual is able to acquire a product or service for less than they would have previously paid, they have additional income which can be invested in other products and services which may further enhance their standard of living.

As technological change erodes the value of existing consumer products, it also chips away at the value of many capital assets.

Before the industrial revolution, most capital was held in the form of land. However, as a result of technological change and in particular the developments in agricultural productivity, the value of agricultural land over the last century has collapsed. This occurred because technology increased the yield that could be obtained from farmland, allowed once marginal land to become productive and opened up global food markets. All of these developments reduced scarcity and subsequently drove down prices. Similar processes will continue to devalue all forms of wealth and productive capital.

All of this erodes the value of pre-existing capital back down to any recoverable material or minimum productive value as seen in our earlier example of agrarian land.

For example, intangible assets such as intellectual property could become next to valueless overnight if the product in question was superseded by a single new dominant technology or if societal changes make the former product undesirable.

Plant and machinery costs could also reduce rapidly. If the market evaporated for the product being manufactured then, unless the factory could be repurposed to produce a new valuable product, the factories value would collapse to the recoverable material price and any intrinsic land value.

Stock held for any period of time may also devalue as new products and services transform consumer desires and expectations.

This process is occurring today but as the rate of change accelerates, the rate at which capital devalues will also accelerate to a point where every asset has to be considered durable.

This in turn means in order to make investment pay, rates of return will need to rise to offer an almost immediate return on investment.

Share value has often been calculated based upon the anticipated profits over a twenty-year period. With the increasing rate of technological and allied social change, this time period will need to be reduced dramatically due to the real threat of an investment becoming worthless when it competes with the products and services of the future.

Technology has been recently tending towards the products which, due to their link with digital technologies, are generally non-rival and can therefore be copied at little cost. This, coupled with improved distribution and communications technologies, have resulted in a global 'winner takes all' economy where the best products are often available to the majority of people on the planet.

However, in a world of ceaseless change, the best is only the best for a small period of time as competitors soon emerge to challenge the dominance of a market leader. Therefore, all of these companies need to constantly refresh and upgrade or risk being superseded by a new challenger business.

This 'winner takes all' trend has further shifted the economic balance in favour of capital and away from labour as workers struggle to obtain significant benefits during the small period of economic gain. This too has allowed capital to claim a larger proportion of the overall profits.

This requirement for a higher rate of return from capital to offset increased risk, disrupts the once fairly stable split between the profits distributed to capital and the profits distributed to labour. As capital has stolen part of the value generated which was once allocated to labour it has started to impact wealth distribution in our society.

This has also been possible due to changes in the labour market set out in chapter three which have generally lessened the power of labour.

The owners of capital cannot indefinitely keep increasing their share of profits. Instead, the only answer to an ever increasing rate of change in a capitalist system is to simultaneously have an ever increasing rate at which products and services will be assimilated into our lives. This does not just require active consumers but a significant change in the consumer-producer relationship. This is particularly the case in the most fast moving of industries.

This new economy is already emerging. A market which no longer sells the ownership of individual products but instead has converted products to services which are accessible through subscription. This is a trend being facilitated by the direction of recent technologies.

Instead of compiling a book or film collection, people now subscribe to a service which gives them instant access to large databases of content from which to choose.

Instead of buying a version of software, people pay a subscription to a particular software package which is constantly developed and improved. More recently, even the purchase of expensive, fashionable clothing and accessories are now made available for selection by consumers subscribed to a designer service.

This ensures customers have immediate access to often cutting edge technology, fashion or content. This speeds up the process at which new designs and developments can be enjoyed and utilised by the end consumer. It also encourages continuous development which in an economy built on individual purchases may not be able to cost effectively produce and distribute small iterative improvements. In addition, it allows producers to achieve price discrimination based on the speed people wish to gain access to certain desirable content or products.

From the businesses standpoint, they will be able to extract the maximum amount of value from each consumer as each person identifies how much they are willing to pay and how long they are willing to wait to gain access to the next generation of developments.

This trend has the potential to transform our concept of poverty. Poverty stops being a measure of what an individual has, or more accurately, what they do not have, but instead it becomes a measure of how long they have to wait to acquire access.

In some sense this is already true. A person considered poor fifty years ago would not have possessed a television or a microwave oven. Nowadays, many people in the western world, who may be far from affluent, own these goods and a number of other products which are improvements on the most desirable commodities of their grandparent's generation.

Therefore, the economic changes being witnessed could be viewed as the reduction of access time to the latest goods and services.

Some may not consider delayed access equating to poverty. This is clearly not a description of absolute poverty, where a person does not have the means to provide adequate, food, clothing, shelter, warmth and clean water. However, it could be considered a form of social poverty where people do not have the resources to fully engage with society. This may seem like a far less concerning form of poverty but it can reduce the opportunity of these individuals, leave them excluded from society and can create a trap from which it is next to impossible to escape.

There may be an opportunity for absolute poverty to be globally eradicated if economic growth and the benefits of this new abundance of wealth are spread more equitably across the planet. Social poverty however will remain and perhaps even increase in magnitude as people struggle to afford to keep up with the pace of change in the modern world. The economic and social consequences of failing to keep up with technological and social trends may be disastrous to an individual's income, future opportunities and social standing.

Nevertheless, not all goods are fungible or easily distributed. Consumer goods, resources which are used up by the consumer, such as fuel or food, clearly will have issues around being offered for access instead of for purchase. Principally, it would remove any incentive to limit consumption of these limited resources as after the subscription was paid there would be no financial incentive not to consume. There would also be a lack of an effective market pricing system to handle supply and demand leading to potential production shortfalls or wastage.

This is not the only situation where a lack of effective markets could be a concern in the future. To function correctly, markets require perfect information within the system to determine supply and demand and to set prices. However, unknown competition from the future and the rapidly changing nature of the market, has inserted a considerable amount of uncertainty into the system.

It is important to distinguish risk from uncertainty. The American Economist, Frank Knight, defined risk as situations where a probability can be assigned precisely to the outcomes. Risks can be assessed, balanced and appropriately priced. Uncertainty however is an unquantifiable and unknowable risk.

Let us assume for a moment all economic participants are able to behave rationally. They assess each possible future, determine the risk and therefore the likelihood of that particular event occurring and its value to them. Using this information, they are able to calculate the expected utility they will receive from a particular transaction. Much of mainstream economics assumes even if economic participants are not undertaking these calculations, they are behaving as if they are. Yet if there is uncertainty in the system, it becomes impossible to calculate the expected utility and with it the optimum outcome and decision.

One aspect of uncertainty in decision making is our inability to conceive of the goods and services which will be available in the future, not to mention all future market conditions or social and political eventualities. Mervin King in his 2016 book, The End of Alchemy, wrote: 'Radical uncertainty drives a gaping hole through the idea of complete and competitive markets. Even if the markets that do exist are competitive, many crucial markets for future goods and services are absent'. He continues 'When IBM launched its personal computer (The PC) in 1981, there were no markets in the products that subsequently displaced it in the consumer marketplace, such as laptop and tablet devices'

In the classical theory of economics, a market is able to self-regulate by interest rates, wages and prices adjusting dynamically to maintain a balance between investments and savings and the supply and demand of products and services.

As this idealised system would always be in balance, it would be impossible that any financial asset would suddenly devalue and induce a financial crisis.

Yet with uncertainty in the system and all these future markets and competing technologies missing, then even if all participants are behaving rationally and are appropriately pricing risk, then market failures may still occur as asset values change quickly and unpredictably as events unfold. This is why John Maynard Keynes, amongst others, believed that it was uncertainty and not the over pricing of risk which tended to lead to a financial crisis.

This should be a concern as the rate of technological and allied social change increases, so does the amount of uncertainty that has to be tolerated within any economic system.

Presently governments often view banks as 'too big to fail' and their assumed support means even if a bank gets into economic difficulties, deposits are often secured. Will this position be sustainable as the banking sector becomes ever more volatile as risk and uncertainty increase?

Not only do banks have to accept the market they operate in will become more uncertain but some of their main practices for generating profits further exacerbate the uncertainty they are exposed to.

In particular, maturity transformation, where banks take on short term liabilities to acquire long term, riskier assets. This process is profitable for banks but in addition to taking on more risk in this manner, this practice also increases the amount of uncertainty the banks are exposed to. This is because, as discussed in Chapter 2, uncertainty increases rapidly the further a projection is made into the future.

In the relatively static world of yesterday, this would not necessarily be a considerable factor. However, in a world of ceaseless change, this will become an ever greater challenge for the banking sector as they attempt to manage this amount of uncertainty within their assets whilst maintaining profits and the trust and confidence of depositors.

These are not the only challenges technological change will bring to our financial systems. As noted in the previous chapter, if the challenges facing the labour market go unaddressed and the present trend continues for a lack of opportunity to acquire and retain skilled work, it will erode our pool of available consumers. Without willing consumers, investments in future technology and job creation become unsustainable and the economy enters a vicious cycle of decline.

Unspectacular growth, increased uncertainty, competition with the future and technological deflation are all threats to capital and our financial system.

The cumulative effect of these forces makes capital just as precarious as labour markets. A system is therefore needed which will help generate growth by providing investment and ensures a functioning market which utilises the knowledge and experience of our entire community. This is the moment to return to the idea introduced in the previous chapter for a Universal Investment.

A Universal Investment would be a regular credit made available to every adult which would be at their disposal to invest however they saw fit in either established or start-up businesses. They would have the right to claim any dividends these investments generated and to even trade or capitalise the shares after some agreed period of time.

Such a proposal would bring about true common ownership without the need for a bulky state apparatus and would allow improved crowd decision making. It would also be a redistributive force that would ensure more people had regular and perhaps substantial incomes that could ensure they could have a good standard of living and could therefore continue to be active consumers. It is also likely to make crowd funding for start-up businesses and other good ideas more widely available.

The political right believes in the power of the market and the political left believe in common ownership. However, this proposal may receive criticism from both sides of the current political divide.

The right may argue some people may not be able to make logical decisions with this investment. This may appear to be a potential problem, however, modern economics recognises efficient economies do not require a group of perfect decision makers, in fact, as an efficient aggregating tool they need a broad range of individuals with different information and outlooks to be successful.

The left may argue the market is inherently an exploitative apparatus and does not work in the interests of working people. However, by putting the market in the hands of the many and not just a financial elite, society may enjoy all the benefits from this new improved and more democratic method to allocate resources and rewards.

Common ownership in practice is generally understood to mean ownership rests with the state or a state run institution which leverages that asset allegedly in the public good. Therefore, perhaps this should instead be described as distributed community ownership which is clearly distinct from common ownership as the ownership rests not in an institution but across a broad section of society. These individual shareholders can collectively bring their creative energies or insights to projects and use these to leverage their ownership stake and generate an improved income for themselves and their families.

Democratising the market and distributing the proceeds to large swathes of the public surely must be an improvement. Instead of seeing quick rewards being made by a few winners, these rewards will be more widely distributed in society.

A market would be created which was more effective at predicting which products or business models will be successful due to the wider pool of information and experiences held by potential investors.

No longer will only wealthy investors or people with the skills to set up certain ground-breaking businesses be the only ones who can use their insights and knowledge to generate wealth in this manner. Instead, anyone who can spot micro-trends at their inception and invest accordingly to exploit these arising opportunities can benefit. Everybody could be an investor in the next Apple, Google or Facebook.

As with all markets there will be winners and losers but this process will be repeated continuously. Therefore, it would give everyone the opportunity to invest wisely or fortunately in the future. Any returns achieved will not be considered handouts. Instead, income received in this manner will have been earnt which will give people the necessary sense of pride and dignity.

The main argument against any form of capital redistribution is the belief money needs to be kept with individuals who will invest it in activities which will drive economic investment.

Assuming a Universal Investment was implemented and such a scheme was funded by a tax on the capital assets of the wealthy, the same amount if not more of this capital would be invested.

Inequality would narrow as everyone would have the opportunity to generate income from labour and income from capital.

The quality of investments would be improved due to information being held in the crowd becoming available to the market at the point of investment and not only at the point the consumer decides.

This would occur as the entire diverse adult population would be using their insights and knowledge to maximise their investments instead of simply the current narrow group of wealthy investors and financiers. This would help unleash additional growth and would help create new jobs.

Finally, it may help deliver better provisions for people in retirement as a considerable number of people would have the benefit of income from capital after their working days were over. This would reduce the burden on the state to provide financial support for people post-retirement.

Of course a tax on capital assets needs to be carefully introduced. Individuals who have worked hard should not have to worry about the security of their homes, pension pots and any modest savings. Therefore, a tax free amount would need to be established to prevent people who have simply worked hard and saved diligently from being lumbered with a potentially considerable annual tax bill.

In the future, wealthy people will still exist. In a global winner takes all market, the amounts of wealth individuals may be able to accrue may be colossal. Yet as a result of ceaseless change, wealth will be far more transient.

The value of once stable assets will erode. Investment and savings will become more uncertain and markets will become less efficient as participation is narrowed to a small number of active traders or perhaps even a handful of super computers trading on our behalf.

Whilst a position of wealth may not be sustainable, action must be taken to allow all participants in our economy to sustain a comfortable and secure lifestyle whilst avoiding social poverty and exclusion. This cannot be achieved by stifling capital but can only occur if capital is directed and put to work for every person in our society and not just a select few.

Chapter 5

Exploring Education and Adapting to Opportunity

As the rate of technological change continues to accelerate, our skills will increasingly devalue, putting our job security at risk.

Significant damage could be done if new jobs are not created as quickly as they are destroyed by waves of innovation. Yet, there is good reason to think in a vibrant economy, new opportunities will continue to be created to replace the jobs which have been destroyed.

However, this is not the only threat to working people who wish to maintain well paid, skilled work. Whilst net job destruction is uncertain, the increased rate of 'career churn' is inevitable.

Already, the expectation of a job for life is quickly diminishing and people will soon all assume they will have a number of different careers throughout their working life. This trend will continue. This is partly a positive outcome as people pursue opportunity and seek to build better careers. However, it is also being driven by ceaseless changes in the job market as our economy and society are constantly restructured around us. Those who can cling on to a single career will find it will be essential to regularly overhaul their own knowledge and skills as the requirements for their job transform fundamentally over time.

It will therefore not be long until the vast proportion of working people need to completely reskill a number of times during their working life in order to maintain skilled employment.

This situation makes the threat to an individual's employability not just about the accessibility and availability of jobs. Instead increasingly an individual's adaptability and the speed at which they can acquire a new skill, trade or profession will largely determine the opportunities they will find available.

Without question this will force the first major change to our educational system. No longer can education be a pursuit undertaken principally when young. Instead, it will be essential to transition to a system where every person engages in lifelong learning and reskilling.

Our existing education system cannot be expected to successfully predict and impart all the skills needed during a working lifetime. Careers will instead consist of a significant number of distinct and perhaps fleeting occupations, many of which would have been unknowable years before when a person embarked upon their educational journey.

Such an educational change would also bring about further fundamental changes to our working lives.

In the modern world, time is a precious resource as people juggle work, community commitments, family responsibilities and personal time. It is therefore unrealistic to assume widespread reskilling could occur 'out of hours' on a vocational basis.

Instead, work will have to comprise of periods of earning and learning to ensure people are maintaining useful skill levels and preparing themselves for the inevitable next career transition.

Just as working people have slowly won the right to paid holiday, the right to career-long paid training release must now be won.

In many professions, this right has already been widely established. Undertaking Continuous Professional Development (CPD) is now often a requirement to maintain the right to practise in a number of fields including medicine and law.

This requirement for lifelong reskilling comes with its own challenges. If the proportion of the working week where people are engaged in productive work decreases, the work undertaken will need to be more productive in order to maintain salaries and the lifestyles to which they are accustomed. Alternatively, labour will have to receive a larger proportion of the proceeds of their productive work.

It will also force some individuals who may have had an unpleasant and unproductive experience of education to overcome negative associations and reengage with the process of learning and reskilling.

As people are forced to regularly switch careers, this will lead to greater uncertainty for families who will be forced to adjust to periods where their household income sharply decreases. This will be the case if individuals opt to re-enter full time education or if they are accepting low skilled work whilst attempting to transition into their next career.

Nevertheless, if education becomes a truly lifelong pursuit, it will break down some of the barriers that exist today for people who fail to flourish under the existing educational system.

Today, many people who enter the workplace with next to no qualifications not only begin their careers with few options but they also find fewer opportunities to improve skills and demonstrate natural talents or abilities. This further limits their opportunities to move up the career ladder.

This is principally because companies, especially those who employ people in low skilled jobs, have little incentive to improve the opportunities of their staff. Their business models demand the employment of low paid and low skilled workers to undertake repetitive tasks. Therefore, upskilling is only likely to increase the rate at which these individuals leave the business, adding to recruitment and basic retraining costs.

This process is not limited to low skilled industries. Many businesses, including those in more high-skill, high value trades and professions, are loathed to develop people who will likely be poached by a competitor. However, by making universal training available to all working people, far more opportunity will open up. Instead of being stuck on the bottom rungs, more people will be able to ascend the career ladder. This can only improve the motivation of countless working people who currently see only a future of drudgery and limited opportunities to build a better life. Failure to make this change will result in a complete reversal of the standard career path. For generations, people generally increased their earning potential throughout their lives. This occurred as they improved and refined their skills over time and built up a considerable amount of experience which made them more valuable to employers.

However, if the opportunity to reskill throughout a working life is denied, it will become more likely people will experience a brief burst of productive work at the start of their careers with opportunity and financial reward decreasing over time as skills became increasingly redundant.

This would inevitably lead to an unskilled and low paid group of older workers who would become less financially secure and independent as they approached retirement age. This does not seem a good system to ensure our senior citizens will have healthy and happy retirements. Instead, older workers will place additional burdens on their family to provide financial and other support.

Education is understandably held up as the solution to these difficulties but the solution isn't as simple as more of the same old educational practises.

Our current educational system, designed in the Victorian era, was created to reproduce the repetitive work of the factory with bells ringing to signal the start of the working day and children organised in rows like production line workers.

If not being prepared for the factory, children were trained to recall and apply a range of knowledge prized in the professions. This system therefore does little more than assess young people's ability to learn and apply fixed rules.

Such skills, whilst once valuable, are now prime candidates to be some of the next tasks to be automated. Information technology, which is ideally adapted for repetitive rule based applications, is becoming increasingly capable in many fields as processing power continues to increase exponentially and natural language processing approaches human levels of comprehension.

For this reason, pressures on employment will soon extend beyond blue collar employment which has already undergone considerable reform through automation.

The professional classes will also face increased competition by new technology. Many of these jobs have been historically well paid and it was therefore understandable the skills needed to undertake these professional tasks were highly regarded. They were therefore prized by society and promoted through the education system.

By simply insisting on more formal education, instead of necessarily increasing aptitude and opportunity for the participants, it may do little more than driving grade inflation as the required level of educational attainment increases to access opportunity.

This is already a visible trend. Many jobs which would have once been open to people who had obtained a vocational qualification or could have been accessed through at work training, are now deemed to require degree level qualifications.

This could be seen as a positive trend if large swathes of the workforce were applying degree level skills within the economy. However, more often these qualifications are used as little more than aptitude tests before people embark on an unrelated or loosely related career.

Despite this increase in degree level candidates, employers continue to complain people entering the workforce do not possess the skills and qualities they desire in modern employees.

The problem however is not that people are undertaking more formal education. This is fundamentally a good thing. The problem instead is our educational institutions, our political decision makers and a large number of employers, remain enthralled with outdated forms of instruction and assessment. Conscientious parents therefore feel compelled to direct their children to focus their energies on passing examinations that they believe will help unlock job opportunities.

This persists despite the fact many aspects of our outdated institutions are not designed, and are in fact incapable of preparing people, for modern working life.

The ability to retain and repeat information, is now no measure of an individual's ability to flourish in modern workplaces and does little to develop important characteristics such as creativity, adaptability and insight.

This is clearly counterproductive as it encourages a culture where people are being taught to the tests in order to maximise results instead of developing skills which will have a productive application in tomorrow's job market.

Despite this deficiency, there is a logic to this approach. More often than not, opportunity is still awarded on these fairly arbitrary scales but this is unsurprising when they are the only scales of performance accredited by the state and the only scale specified by employers.

Successful people in today's society are people who succeeded under the old outdated education system based on core subjects and standardised testing.

Whilst some individuals may have flourished under this system, it doesn't mean the school population as a whole positively applied their talents. Nor does it mean the economy was provided with the best candidates for all possible opportunities.

It is important to point out those individuals who went on to achieve additional success, usually did so because their skills have been improved and augmented by their wider work and life. They have acquired their skills in other environments and have often succeeded in spite of their education, not as a result of it. Even if they still apportion credit to the institutions they passed through as young people those institutions only provided the basic building blocks for learning and some have been more effective in that role than others.

The present system does have some value. Students invest their time, intellect and ability into their work and this is converted into an easily comparable grade that can be converted into opportunities for well-paid work.

A clear transaction is taking place that is understood across society. This system, having clear steps and a sense of fair reward, makes it an attractive scheme and a hard one to replace.

Therefore, opportunity is still awarded on these arbitrary and outdated measures and the system does little to ensure the maximum amount of creativity is unleashed and talents are fully harnessed. Unlocking the creative potential of every individual, must become the aim of our new educational system.

The educationalist, Ken Robinson, writes in his 2009 book, The Element: 'The world is changing faster than ever in our history. Our best hope for the future is to develop a new paradigm of human capacity to meet a new era of human existence. We need to evolve a new appreciation of the importance of nurturing human talent along with an understanding of how talent expresses itself differently in every individual. We need to create environments – in our schools, in our workplaces and in our public offices – where every person is inspired to grow creatively. We need to make sure that all people have the opportunity to do what they should be doing, to discover the Element in themselves and in their own way.'

To be clear, this is not an issue about changes to the curriculum. The nature of the next technological or social epoch is largely unknowable and therefore it is impossible to build a curriculum which prepares a generation for the employment opportunities of tomorrow.

Instead, people need to be provided with the tools to discover their passion so they are able to unleash their natural aptitude.

When it comes to education, one size does not fit all. Over recent years, there have been a number of moves in different nations to adapt and reform the Victorian style education system and create more individual learning environments.

In the UK for example, new academies have been introduced. Academies were designed to take secondary schools and colleges out of state control and instead allow parents along with religious, business and community leaders to invest in and shape the education of their children.

The main areas of opposition related to the lack of oversight, the removal of collective bargaining for teaching and school support staff and finally the trend towards employing people who were not trained teachers to deliver lessons.

Putting these concerns aside, this approach had a number of challenges. These prevented this policy from creating a truly adaptable institution which could adjust to meet the individual needs of our children in a world of constant change.

The introduction of academies was designed to provide parents with choice. In theory, parents could select from a range of varied educational opportunities available to their children. This was intended to allow parents to be able to select and shape the correct learning style and setting for their child.

If successful, this would create market conditions where only the successful institutions which attracted pupils would be sustained. Institutions which offered poorer or simply outdated educational opportunities would lose this competitive battle and would be replaced by more suitable institutions.

However, there are a number of reasons why this system fails when the theory collides with reality.

The principal problem is schools are not available to any young person wherever they may be. Geographical and other choice limiting factors will prevent people truly picking the best educational opportunities for their child and therefore this will prevent a true market forming.

Most people would want the best possible education on their doorstep, firstly for convenience but also so the child didn't have the burden of staying away from home or being transported across the country, not to mention the additional financial implications to access these opportunities. Secondly, the people shaping these institutions and the parents making the decision on the best options for their children remain heavily skewed towards achieving traditional grades assessed on the ability to retain and repeat information. As discussed, this is however no measure of a pupil's ability to flourish in modern workplaces and effectively use skills such as creativity, adaptability and insight.

Strong incentives also exist to encourage institutions to persist with delivering a rote learnt curriculum in order to maximise pupil's test results.

This lack of true choice removes any opportunity for this initiative to produce a virtuous circle of constant improvement and adaptation in our educational system.

Instead, a system remains which has all the challenges around oversight and professionalism listed previously without any of the benefits of a system which was truly able to meet the changing needs of our children. It could also be argued that young people are best placed to make decisions about the focus of their education instead of their parents. Adults find it easy to assume they know best for their children and particularly in their early years this is still clearly the case. However, there would be clear advantages to allowing young people to have more control over the direction of their own educational journey.

In Alvin Tofler's book, Future Shock, he extends the idea of 'culture shock'. Culture shock is the feeling of uncertainty experienced when somebody finds themselves in the midst of an unfamiliar culture. Tofler suggested that this feeling would increasingly apply to people in the future as the world and their once familiar culture transforms around them due to the driving forces of technological change.

Tofler writes: '[Culture shock] is what happens when the familiar psychological cues that help an individual function in society are suddenly withdrawn and are replaced by new ones that are strange or incomprehensible. Yet culture shock is relatively mild in comparison to the much more serious malady, future shock. Future shock is the dizzying disorientation brought on by the premature arrival of the future.'

Young people are often far abler to adapt to their surroundings. When families emigrate to new nations with a different cultural identity, it is often the children who first adapt to the new way of life and help assimilate their parents to the new culture.

It should therefore be expected that young people would be the first to adapt to new technologies, adapt to cultural expectations and identify new opportunities. It is not hard to conclude there is some merit in this analysis when young people display a natural aptitude for emerging technology whilst the previous generation struggle to adapt and keep pace with these changes.

As the world changes around us, young people will adapt and thrive and will be best placed to recognise emerging opportunities. In contrast, the older generations will become more economically and socially isolated as they struggle to adapt to technological change. Are these the people who should be making decisions about the priorities for the next generation's education?

Young people will quickly assimilate to societal changes and will adapt their behaviour and aspirations accordingly. They will be better placed to recognise where opportunity may lie and they will have a better chance of identifying their element and properly exploiting their natural talents and aptitudes.

Their decisions may not always be perfect but mistakes should not be feared but instead seen as part of the process of achieving the optimum skills mix in society.

By taking responsibility for their educational choices, they will be learning an additional important lesson about the importance of personal development and putting all their natural abilities to good use.

It is true some may not seize this opportunity but as learning becomes a lifelong pursuit, everyone will always have the opportunity to build upon their skills and open up new avenues to productive work.

If these important changes are made, the door will never shut on educational opportunities. However, by seizing them earlier in life, people will earn a head start as they compete to find productive applications for their natural and developed talents.

In the past, a parent's assistance guiding their child through their educational journey would have been helpful as the world would be relatively unchanged. Through a parent's or guardian's own experiences, successes and mistakes, they would have a good understanding of how to gain access to a number of profitable opportunities. By passing on their knowledge, they would help their children successfully navigate the career maze and perhaps gain an advantage.

Nowadays, advice built upon outdated insights and experiences will no longer be useful. It may be hard for some to accept that a young person with limited experience should be given agency over their education and career, but advice should be limited to encouraging hard work and creative expression.

Despite perhaps the right intentions, the UK approach to delivering a more adaptable education system has failed.

Therefore, instead of having numerous institutions which offer different educational journeys, a system where every school and college offers a personalised learning experience for each child or adult learner should be embraced.

A culture of flexibility, choice and creativity should be instilled into secondary, tertiary and adult education. Individual learners should be able to choose bespoke roles in projects facilitated by schools, colleges and universities. Working either independently or as part of a team, they should be given the freedom to explore all of the educational opportunities available, pursue their passions and follow their insights about how such talents could be applied in the modern world.

There are already a number of such institutions. SOLE schools (Self Organised Learning Environments) along with institutions which practise the famous Montessori Method of Education have been in use across the globe for over 100 years.

However, whilst exploring education is vitally important, in order to be creative in a subject, a technical proficiency must first be obtained. For example, if an individual has never been taught the technical aspects of the violin, it would be extremely difficult for them to be truly creative with the instrument.

When people think about creativity in education, they often turn their mind to the arts. Painting, sculpture, dance, drama and music jump immediately to mind. However, in the modern economy, creativity has to be a key component in every aspect of our working lives and therefore our education.

For example, both mathematics and the sciences are seen by many as having few creative opportunities and are instead an exercise in retaining and recalling theories and formulas. On the contrary, mathematics, like the violin, is the instrument that must be mastered to allow the creation of exciting representations of the physical world.

Einstein, for example, imagined numerous creative thought experiments to allow him to unlock the secrets of the universe which he was able to capture and express in the beautiful language of mathematics.

So skills need to go hand in hand with creative expression and discovery of these topics and technology may hold the answer. Whilst still in their infancy, MOOCS, Massive Online Open Courses, webinars and other e-learning options may be the first expressions of the eventual answer. Despite early promise, these online interactive learning platforms have been slow to take off. Partly because they are not generally offered as part of a formal education and recognised qualifications are rarely provided. In addition, individual's time constraints make it difficult to fit such activities around the pressures associated with family and work.

If these resources and tools are going to help reshape our educational system, it will be necessary that they are incorporated into a more formal education with a recognised system for acknowledging the participant's achievements. Perhaps therefore, a future educational model may resemble the following:

Students and other lifelong learners should, with the guidance of their tutor, select suitable interactive MOOCS delivered by some of the best educators in the nation, if not the world. Pupils should be encouraged to select courses which both build up necessary skills but also ignite their interest and passions.

Completion of one MOOC would immediately open up new suggested areas of knowledge exploration. Perhaps, modelling algorithms similar to those used by Amazon to suggest appropriate book purchases to their customers, could identify interesting and suitable courses for individuals to undertake.

Instead of being robotically tested on a defined list of learning outcomes and graded on recalling factual snippets of these courses, students in our system will receive an accreditation when they successfully and uniquely apply the skill in order to demonstrate a competence in their project work. Such a system would better model how information is acquired an applied in real world scenarios.

The old grade system which has had a value to both the students and the wider economy, will still exist but instead of the need to undertake tests and assessments, these new grades will be formed by banding the number of skills that have been proficiently demonstrated by topic.

For example, if a student had appropriately demonstrated a considerable number of mathematical skills, this will correspond to a high achieved grade. By institutionalising lifelong learning, participants would constantly have the opportunity to enhance these achieved grades as they continue to acquire and apply skills through work or lifelong learning courses.

Schools and colleges would work to design and support up to date and relevant project opportunities. These would be designed to develop a multitude of talents that draw on a wide range of knowledge and skills. It would also be advantageous for these institutions to encourage people to interact with individuals with different skills and talents in order to appreciate the importance of collaboration. These again are vital skills in the modern workplace which educational institutions would mirror.

By seeking out the correct collaborators who can help develop and improve their work, they would also demonstrate an appreciation of the skills of others.

Such collaborations don't necessarily need to be limited to one educational institution or within age groups. Assuming appropriate safeguarding was in place, why shouldn't collaboration be encouraged with people at university or with people undertaking training as part of their universal educational opportunity through work?

This would avoid students being left with a narrow band of potential collaborators and would build a network which they could exploit to help find suitable employment in the future.

By advertising for and identifying suitable collaborators, people could find kindred spirits who share an interest which may even have the potential to develop into longstanding working relationships. Perhaps once again technology will play a role where our ideal collaborators are identified in the same way as modern dating apps introduce people to their future romantic partners. Could the next Steve Jobs find the next Steve Wosniak in such a way?

This would allow the cross fertilisation of ideas, open up new creative possibilities across the entire educational network and drive additional creativity and economic growth.

Students would benefit greatly by being encouraged to instigate and develop independent projects of their own. Just like at Google, where employees were able to dedicate up to 20% of their time to their own projects, students at all levels should be encouraged to collaborate on, and develop, their own ideas.

Such a measure will help students recognise that innovation and creativity are often both individual and group pursuits. Where they see gaps in their own skill, they would be able to address these by undertaking the appropriate courses and also by learning directly from fellow group members.

Learning directly from peers should not be discounted as a method of education as a large proportion of our skills and knowledge are acquired from engaging with friends, associates and colleagues.

Having undertaken a course or not, skills acquired this way should also be acknowledged by our proposed grading system if a student is able to correctly demonstrate their application through paid or project work.

There are three potential barriers to such a system taking root.

Parents may not be willing to cede control to their children. Employers may not recognise and value these new style qualifications and testing regimes and finally, students and life-long learners may not be confident, by committing to this new educational system, opportunity would be there for them at the end of the process.

However, strong leadership in both government and in the business community should allay many of the concerns of parents and students alike. This would especially be so if a cross party consensus could be achieved ensuring such reforms were not likely to be quickly overhauled.

Just as the Victorians created an educational system which produced production line workers and human computation machines, our generation must create an education system which produces creative, collaborative and adaptable workers perfect for this new change economy.

Education is one of life's most important investments. However, it is increasingly the case these investments are not paying off for young people.

This is because it is increasingly a broken market. Out of control grade inflation has dramatically increased the initial required investment of time. These investments are also no longer as stable. People are increasingly finding their skills rarely required or redundant after only a small window of moderate financial return.

Finally, the current recession in opportunity, caused by constant competition against a growing global market of skilled workers and improvements in algorithms and automation, will undermine investor confidence.

This risks seriously dis-incentivising education and the acquisition of knowledge and skills. If skills quickly diminish or if gaining a fleeting opportunity involves entering an extremely competitive market, some may conclude the time and effort needed to invest in acquiring skills will not be worth the limited rewards.

Yet only by investing in their personal development will people avoid slipping back into the pool of unskilled work. If they allow this to happen they will end up competing for low waged work against both increased automation and a constantly renewed pool of the once-skilled unemployed.

However, the education and jobs market can transform to instil personal choice, wide participation and clear incentives for making the correct decisions. This individual investment approach will help deliver skills and applied knowledge that will match job opportunities.

Developing talents and skills and linking these with appropriate employment is effectively an optimisation problem. This is a problem that is nowhere near being solved using the current top down system of prescribed learning.

That being said, if the decision making ability of crowds is utilised it should be possible to ensure a considerable number of people can direct their passions and natural talents to skilled productive labour.

In any market situation there are often winners and losers. Whilst that might be difficult for some to accept, it is clearly already the case in our existing system which selectively offers rewards on the basis of a student's ability to conform to certain classical standards.

By ensuring access to lifelong learning, no-one risks becoming educationally bankrupt even if they invest unwisely or unfortunately in their youth.

Everyone will constantly have access to their next educational investment which, if directed correctly, could open up considerable new opportunities, even if mistakes and unforeseen errors occurred in the past. Secondly, the system proposed will not only help develop individual skills but it will drive creativity and entrepreneurship. This will in turn mean additional job creation and with that the opportunities people need to find a productive application for their skills. More and more people will become winners as opportunity growth returns to the market.

Not only will the education received by students be transformed but so will the role of the teacher. Gone will be the hours of lesson planning and delivery. Instead, teaching will become principally about mentoring and guiding students as they pursue their own educational journey. Teachers will provide support if students falter or struggle to understand certain points and assist them to overcome particular challenges.

To see the full benefits of this proposal, a change in business culture is also needed. A culture must be established in organisations where employees are not considered as costs but as assets on their balance sheets. This transforms training from a cost to an organisation to an investment which will increase their staff asset value.

Constant change could have a big impact upon company value. It makes intellectual property less valuable as there would be an increased risk of the protected technology being quickly superseded by competitors. Many products held for even the shortest of periods become outdated which writes off the value of stock. Any plant and machinery that cannot be quickly repurposed and put to new productive work can become valueless. In an extreme world of constant change, the only value which exists within a business would be the collective creative abilities and drive of the organisation's employees along with the systems that allow them to work together effectively.

If reformed correctly, education can be the solution to the new challenges around work. This will not be achieved by simply demanding ever higher levels of attainment but instead by producing free thinking and adaptable employees for organisations of the future. Only their collective vision and creativity will ensure the company has a future and therefore a value to investors.

The adaptability in this proposed education system does not come from constant changes to our educational institutions. Instead, it ensures the institution gets out of the way of many parts of educational decision making and puts these decisions back in the hands of the student or person undertaking life-long learning.

This newly acquired flexibility will ensure people can build the education they want. They will be able to exploit the apparent opportunities and prepare themselves for the new world they find themselves in.

The system proposed is designed to allow learners of all ages, backgrounds and talents to shape the education they receive, to fulfil their potential and to exploit the opportunities they predict will arise. This gives this system huge flexibility and an ability to unleash people with skills that will vary in accordance with changes in the technological, economic and social environment.

Chapter 6

A New Social and Political Epoch

'It is not enough that you should understand about applied science in order that your work may increase man's blessings. Concern for the man himself and his fate must always form the chief interest of all technical endeavours; concern for the great unsolved problems of the organisation of labour and the distribution of goods in order that the creations of mind shall be a blessing and not a curse to mankind. Never forget this in the midst of your diagrams and equations.' Albert Einstein 1933.

The world was once stable. It was never static but change was so slow that to all appearances the world would be unaltered within an individual lifetime. This gave the illusion of a state of permanence to the present. That misconception has now been dispelled and now our politics must recognise this fact and, along with our economy and society, it must become far more fluid in response to this new rate of change.

A manifesto remains a fixed platform to present to the electorate with ideas which could span decades in their discussion, deliberation and implementation.

Our institutions are unchanging monuments to an age gone by. These organisations often actively counteract change as they focus on sustaining themselves in spite of social and political pressure.

Our education system, established with the goal of producing more numerate and literate workers to meet the needs in the age of industrial empires has altered little to meet the demands of the age of change. Stable and dependable career paths once lay before young workers who obtained a skill which in all likelihood they could practise unaltered throughout their working lives. This is no longer the case.

In stark contrast, the market has been the dynamic feature of the modern world. This dynamism, couple with the creative ability of mankind, has driven technological development and has supercharged the transformation of our society.

Akin to King Canute, a minority have tried to stifle economic systems through central control and other repressive measures to hold back the tide of change. They have of course failed. More often, well-meaning people have tinkered with our economic systems in an attempt to make them more equitable. Such interventions have often been delicate touches as most recognise the importance of maintaining the energy, vitality and efficiency of this system.

The aim of building a fairer more equitable society with widespread opportunity is a noble goal and one that should never be lost sight of. To achieve this aim in a world of rapid change, we must strive to make our political and social institutions fluid. This will allow economic dynamism and creativity to be matched with ever increasing social and political dynamism.

By providing the institutions, tools and structures to allow society to respond rapidly to changes, the resistance which has been gently slowing the rate of technological advance will be reduced. This will bring about additional acceleration in the rate of growth as the processes of innovation, development and the adoption of these new ideas becomes almost frictionless. The only remaining resistance will be individual psychological aversion to rapid change as people battle the shock and confusion associated with an unfamiliar world.

Some may conclude a small amount of gentle drag on the forces of change would be beneficial as it would give everybody additional time to acclimatise to the changes which were taking place around them.

This is the case today. Not through design but often through ignorance and outdated practises. Institutional resistance, barriers to trade, constricted money supplies and old-fashioned educational practises are leading to the suboptimal use of our collective talents and skills and are all forces of drag which are limiting the rate of change.

Whilst the creation of new opportunities may be stunted, other processes, which are already resulting in significant and rapid transformations, seem to be far less affected by the present levels of institutional resistance. This apparent asymmetry has been driven by two disruptive forces.

Firstly, as the world has become more interconnected, once stable barriers to trade, collaboration and the free flow of ideas and interactions, have collapsed.

This has opened up global labour markets which have placed considerable downward pressure on wages as economies with low cost labour have opened up and flooded the market with a surplus of low wage workers. This has resulted in jobs, initially in manufacturing and more recently in the service sector, being relocated from the developed world to every corner of the globe.

The second disruptive trend is automation. Just a few years ago it was assumed only repetitive manual tasks in controlled environments were at risk from automation.

However, with the developments in AI, robotics and natural language processing, more jobs are coming under pressure from technological alternatives. This is not only occurring in manufacturing but increasingly in the service sector and the established professions.

Instead of fighting these forces, barriers must be removed to allow the unbridled pace of change to create as many opportunities as possible, as quickly as possible.

Only this way will the jobs and industries be created to replace the jobs which are being haemorrhaged through these processes. Succumbing to fear and erecting Luddite barriers and constraints will be disastrous.

Instead the destruction associated with rapid change must be combatted with ever rising rates of creativity.

However, this approach is not without its challenges. As the rate of creativity and development increases, so does the amount of creative destruction society must tolerate.

In order to stay ahead of the increasing waves of destruction, the rate of technological development must also accelerate to replace the jobs, opportunity and economic value being destroyed.

Clearly, such an undertaking cannot continue indefinitely, so how will this process end?

Perhaps it would be safe to assume this process would have concluded when nearly every worker has transitioned from task based employment to creative or research based employment.

If this process was completed, there would cease to be any workers which were economically under threat from the processes of automation or offshoring.

Working people would not be immune to change as they would still need to adapt by regularly updating their knowledge and adjusting the focus of their creativity but the asymmetry in the system would have disappeared with new opportunities arising as existing forms of productive work were disrupted.

This creative economy would only be under threat if the creative process has been widely automated. This is not inconceivable as algorithms have begun to deliver impressive results in areas such as music composition. However, it is far from certain these or similar technologies will significantly diminish human opportunities for creativity.

Even If every individual was engaged in creative pursuits, our maximum collective creative capacity would not have been reached. The rate of creativity is not exclusively determined by the total number of minds dedicated to creative thought. It is also determined by the tools that are at our disposal to help our creative expressions. Leonardo Da Vinci required a paintbrush to create the Mona Lisa. Without a chisel, Michelangelo could not have uncovered David from the block of marble and if Beethoven had not been introduced to the piano, he could not have produced the haunting melody in Fur Elise.

It is therefore nothing new when the creative ability of an individual or group is augmented or supplemented by tools. This applies even if the tool is as simple as a paintbrush or as advanced as machines capable of observing patterns and extracting new insights from gigantic data sets. Just like other tools have done throughout the ages, modern tools enhance and support our creative work and as our tools improve, they will continue to help increase our creative potential.

However, some people have considered a scenario where the tools can operate without human involvement and many have mused about how our species remains relevant in a world of automatic creativity.

Should this situation ever occur then the technological singularity, first proposed by the 20th century polymath John von Neumann, has been reached.

At this point a future technological intelligence would be able to constantly enhance its own abilities by finding creative technological solutions to its own limitations. As a result, change could occur so inconceivably quickly it would not be possible to comprehend the impact upon human civilisation.

Such a development would clearly bring about a subsequent political epoch and it is therefore beyond the scope of our imaginations and this book which instead remains concerned about the politics of a world shaped by growing human creativity.

In Chapter Two, we explored decision making in an age of rapid change and uncertainty.

Systems were discussed which could aggregate and utilise the knowledge and insights of every member of our society to produce high quality predictions of the future. Better predictions would allow pre-emptive steps to be taken to mitigate fast moving and destructive change.

For example, a system which allowed tax payers to allocate their personal taxable income to government programmes of their choice was proposed. In theory, this would allow competition and dynamic changes to produce the services which were optimised for maximum social benefit. This is unlike the process of privatisation which often just maximises shareholder wealth.

By introducing such a measure, a process would be created which would democratise the allocation of state resources. This is in stark contrast to the present system of handing this responsibility to a chosen few who utilise our collective resources to meet their political aims and objectives and to sustain their own political powerbase.

In Chapter Three and Chapter Four, it was argued the accelerating rate of technological change and the scale of the disruption throughout every sector of our economy makes it extremely difficult for individuals to invest their time wisely in order to acquire a valuable skill.

Due to these new inherent risks associated with attempting to leverage knowledge or labour, systems were discussed which could make capital investment available to the many.

A process is needed which democratises investment so there is a more equitable distribution of opportunity and wealth and also better decision making by having a more diverse group of decision makers.

In Chapter Five, the role education has to play in ensuring people are properly equipped to tackle the ever quickening march of change was examined.

It was proposed that steps should be taken to make education a truly lifelong pursuit to ensure every person of working age had the opportunity to reskill and thus adapt to the new jobs market.

The chapter reviewed how the education system could move away from a heavily structured curriculum and standardised testing to allow individuals to explore their own educational journey.

Once again this is a democratising process where education is not only a pursuit for the young but an essential component throughout an individual's working life. This transfer of power and control to the individual is increasingly evident when the dictatorship of the curriculum and standardised test results, which presently have to be obtained to access opportunity, is removed.

In the future, people must pursue their interests and passions as they seek out not only financially beneficial work but also work which will keep them interested, motivated and happy.

This need to adopt policies which transfer power to a wide and diverse group is the common thread running through this book.

In such a volatile world there are no eternal policy solutions to respond to the march of change. However, if decision making is increasingly decentralised and widely distributed amongst a diverse cross-section of society, it will likely be a step in the right direction.

It is essential to draw upon the collective wisdom of the crowd and aggregate societies' collective knowledge and opinions effectively to ensure good political prediction and decision making.

This will require a method of aggregation that is dynamic and therefore far quicker than the slow pace of collective decision making in many democratic organisations.

Fortunately, the direction technology has been moving in over the last quarter century, lends itself perfectly to this task.

Platforms and networks provide the opportunity for people to easily come together, share information, collaborate and make decisions.

Facebook now provides many people across the globe with a large proportion of the media they consume yet Facebook do not produce any content of their own. Instead, they maintain a platform which allows people to interact to share their thoughts and creativity.

Similarly, to facilitate this democratisation of society, future platforms will be required which help collate our individual knowledge and wisdom without implanting any ideology, insights or preconceptions from the creators or commissioners of this tool.

Just as Facebook allows the exchange of thoughts, experiences and personal creativity, tools will be required which can aggregate our collective opinions and insights effectively whilst providing meaningful feedback and suitable incentives for participation.

To some such systems, particularly if they were controlled by companies, the state or powerful individuals, may appear primed for manipulation. However, there are a number of reasons why platforms should be resistant to any attempts to influence the political process.

Firstly, platforms which fail to maintain trust will cease to have active and engaged participants. Secondly, the purpose of such platforms is to help improve the speed and quality of the decision making process. Assuming competition between nations, a state utilising a platform which skewed the insights of their citizens to benefit a minority would be put at a significant competitive disadvantage. There would therefore be economic and social pressure to keep the system open, honest and free from coercion or distortion.

Such tools could therefore be considered as modern and dynamic equivalents to the nineteenth century technology of the ballot box.

The need to reform and rebuild our institutions to make them more adaptable has been a theme running throughout this book. Yet in certain circumstances, technology may be able to remove all institutional friction by removing the need for the institution all together.

Take the example of Bit Coin. Bit Coin was conceived in a 2008 paper by an individual or group writing under the name Satoshi Nakamoto as a currency which did not require a central authority, such as a bank or a state, to administer or oversee transactions.

This new cryptocurrency was built around the central innovation of the block chain. The block chain is a secure public ledger which permanently records each transaction which took place in the system. This prevents individuals from spending their digital currency more than once.

Tools such as the block chain therefore have the potential to maintain trust within diverse, disparate and often anonymous communities without the need for a formal institution to manage or adjudicate upon interactions within the system.

This therefore can replace static, unchanging institutions with an emergent and dynamic structure which, instead of being imposed upon the system, can instead arise from the actions of individual members of the community.

As well as removing some of the institutional barriers to change, we must also explore the possibility of fully utilising technology to assist with political decision making.

Many important decisions have already been shifted away from people to algorithms to help improve accuracy and consistency and this process has been happening for some time.

In order to qualify for a personal or business loan, there is no longer a need to try to persuade a local bank manager but instead the availability of credit is based entirely on an individual's credit score.

A credit score is little more than the output from an algorithm which assesses the statistical likelihood of an individual repaying a loan. Therefore, this can be used to automatically determine if a loan is approved, denied or alternatively it can set the terms at which a loan can be made.

Another example is the use of deep learning systems to undertake medical diagnosis. In particular, efforts to help diagnose early signs of cancerous tumours have been highly successful. However, despite these results, due to the current preference for human involvement, pathologists are still used to oversee the results.

If the transfer of billions of pounds and even critical diagnoses can be handed over successfully to machines, it is not inconceivable in the future some aspects of political decision making may be transferred to specialist systems.

As our lives become even more connected with our devices recording, monitoring and collecting data about every action and interaction, more accurate statistical models could be produced to describe our opinions and world view.

One of the risks that may be encountered through transferring more decision making back to the individual is that the process of constant contribution may become too onerous.

The joy of a market approach is, through simply expressing one's preferences, a considerable amount of useful information emerges which helps mould production and helps set appropriate prices. Tools with similar properties are needed which do not impinge on our time that otherwise could be spent on leisure activities, learning or creative pursuits. Therefore, there is room for tools which provide assistance in this process if society is willing to cede some tasks and control in exchange for time and freedom.

This is not a call for central planning through a single 'mind' being fed information through millions of interconnected sensors and devices. As demonstrated by economist Frederick Hayek, attempts to have centrally planned systems encounter problems due to lack of information.

Clearly, improvements in technology and the fact many of us now carry devices around packed with an array of sensors which monitor many of our actions, has increased the amount of data which can be collected. However, despite this new abundance of information, it remains incomplete.

Having noted this concern and whilst cautioning against putting too much faith in such centralised data there is perhaps a role for people to let algorithms assume some of the burden of the decision making process.

Such a tool, could perhaps monitor messages, conversations and interactions to make projections on their user's political opinions. This would help people communicate their political outlook whilst still giving the individual the opportunity to review, amend and to correct any errors which may have arisen from the model.

Put another way, the device would use its observations of a person's actions and choices to make a number of proposals which could be accepted or rejected by the user. The tool may direct the individual to information they may find useful or relevant or which may help support or challenge their preconceptions. Control would remain with the user as they would be able to make necessary amendments and through this process of feedback, the system could learn to better reflect the individual's views and opinions.

One application of such an approach could relate to the proposal introduced in Chapter Two regarding the funding of public programmes. It was proposed that this function could be handed back to the crowd by allowing individuals to allocate a proportion of their taxable income to the programmes which they believed would be the most beneficial to themselves, their family and their community.

Even if it was clearly worthwhile for society and good incentives were in place, people may be put off from participating if this process became onerous. If people were not spending the requisite amount of time to consider the choices they were making, this system would become inaccurate, unresponsive and could very well lead to poor outcomes.

Therefore, any technological solution that was capable of modelling and extrapolating the personal preferences of the user would potentially streamline the decision making process. This would help ensure the success of future dynamic methods of resource allocation.

As recently as a decade ago, the communications networks required to constantly collate the preferences of millions of people spread across a nation or the tools to help those people contribute effectively to this process were inconceivable.

New political mechanisms must be devised which fully utilise these new and emerging tools to help us keep up with the rate of technological and allied social change.

It would be foolish to predict how these tools and platforms will develop or for that matter what new technologies are on the horizon which may offer solutions to our modern political dilemmas. However, if these trends continue and the world becomes more interconnected and society has the courage to embrace new tools, we will be better placed to respond to any challenges which may come our way.

Whilst technology may indeed provide some tools to help tackle the challenges of ceaseless change by helping our society to become more responsive, let us not forget each individual technology also has the potential to cause its own disruption, the nature of which cannot be predicted.

Before the industrial revolution, could anybody have foreseen climate change? Before the invention of the car, could the traffic jam have been predicted? Before the invention of the internet, could anyone have conceived of the growing number of cybercrimes which are now prevalent?

These challenges arise and will continue to arise and many will have a profound impact upon our communities and our wider society.

For each future change, an individual and timely reaction will be required and none of these solutions are contained within the pages of this book. Instead, this book simply looks at how future societies can be structured to help deliver social progress alongside the inevitable technological developments.

The British philosopher, Bertrand Russell, remarked: 'Change is one thing, progress is another. Change is scientific, progress is ethical; change is indubitable, whereas progress is a matter of controversy.'

Luddite doctrines are dangerous as they repress change but a laissez-fait approach also allows for the considerable risk of change without progress. That being said, whilst huge challenges will arise in the years ahead, these are not challengers which have been forced upon us by another group of people.

This is not a battle between left and right or between different nation states. It is not a battle between different creeds, cultures or religions. This is a battle against some of the unavoidable, negative and destructive consequences of change.

However, whilst change will cause this disruption, it isn't our enemy, in fact change is our big hope for the future. Our enemy, if there is one, is ignorance of the changes taking place and reshaping our societies around us.

It is also important to remain alert to Luddite doctrines which allow people to reject or oppose changes which they are incapable of stopping and which fundamentally represses the fruits of human freedom and creativity.

If a political approach built on acknowledging and adapting to change is adopted, the opportunity exists to put aside the politics of blame. No longer will problems be the fault of the immigrant, the millionaire, the scrounger or the capitalist. It will not be the fault of the bureaucrat, trade unionist or the business owner. Instead, our focus can remain on addressing the negative consequences and disruptive forces unleashed by change within our society. Such difficult challenges will only be overcome together if all of our collective knowledge and skills are utilised to address the big challenges of the day.

This book does not contain any mystical, pre-emptive knowledge about what the future will bring. The ideas proposed should not be thought of as a permanent blueprint for success but instead a few tentative steps which may be beneficial as the journey begins into the unknown where ceaseless change will define a new era.

The forces driving change can no longer be stopped nor would it be in our interests to stop them. Instead society must adapt.

Our way of life, our institutions and our politics must be adjusted to make sure whatever form the future takes, it is a future which works for society as a whole. Failure to do this will risk a collision with a future within which opportunity and prosperity have both dramatically declined.

The industrial revolution transformed our economy and our society and these tides of change which this process unleashed are still the driving force behind the change apparent today.

This revolution occurred in the place and time it did, not as a result of chance and not because a number of talented people developed transformative technology simultaneously. Instead, this transformation occurred because Britain at this time had a unique set of institutions which encouraged this creativity to take place.

Britain's pre-industrial large mercantile class along with earlier battles to decrease monarchical power had helped encourage a more democratic system of open trade and commerce.

Over two centuries later, many variants of these institutions have been implemented across the globe and therefore this culture of innovation, creativity and speculation is now driving accelerating global change. However, these institutions are now over two hundred and fifty years old and were designed for a world that has seen dramatic transformations. It is therefore essential to look at our institutions to understand how they can be made more dynamic and adaptable.

If these changes are made to our institutions, it could potentially unleash a new economic and social revolution that will make industrial and post industrial economies look pedestrian by comparison.

The first states which become early adopters of such measures will immediately possess an advantage and could be propelled to be the next world power. Then, just as the British and later the United States institutional models have been adopted across the globe, these new dynamic institutions will be replicated and implemented as people react to keep up with this new era of progress, prosperity, opportunity and hope.

Printed in Great Britain
by Amazon